NORMAL

NORMAL

ONE KID'S EXTRAORDINARY JOURNEY

YOUNG READERS' EDITION

BY MAGDALENA AND NATHANIEL NEWMAN
WITH HILARY LIFTIN

ILLUSTRATED BY NEIL SWAAB

HOUGHTON MIFFLIN HARCOURT

BOSTON NEW YORK

hmhbooks.com

The text was set in Univers Lt Std and Stempel Garamond.
Typography by Celeste Knudsen

Library of Congress Cataloging-in-Publication Data
Names: Newman, Magdalena M., author. | Newman, Nathaniel, author. | Liftin, Hilary, author. | Swaab, Neil, illustrator.
Title: Normal / by Magdalena M. and Nathaniel Newman, with Hilary Liftin ; illustrated by Neil Swaab. Description: Young Readers edition. | Boston ; New York : Houghton Mifflin Harcourt, [2020] | Audience: Ages 10+ | Audience: Grades 7 to 8. Identifiers: LCCN 2019006110 (print) | LCCN 2019013401 (ebook) | ISBN 9780358164418 (E-book) | ISBN 9781328631831 (hardcover) Subjects: LCSH: Facial bones Abnormalities—Biography—Juvenile literature. | Newman, Nathaniel—Juvenile literature. | Newman, Magdalena M.—Juvenile literature. | Treacher Collins syndrome—Biography—Juvenile literature. | Genetic disorders—Biography—Juvenile literature. | Mothers and sons—Juvenile literature. | Families—Washington (State)—Seattle—Juvenile literature. | Seattle (Wash.)—Biography—Juvenile literature.
Classification: LCC QM695.F32 (ebook) | LCC QM695.F32 N49 2020 (print) | DDC 617.5/20092—dc23
LC record available at https://lccn.loc.gov/2019006110

Manufactured in the United States of America
DOC 10 9 8 7 6 5 4 3 2 1
4500784263

Swimming

NATHANIEL In the summer of 2017 when we got to Beaver Lake, I ran straight into the water. I was wearing a big Spider-Man floaty—but only because it was a very deep lake. I paddled out as far as I could, as fast as I could, singing to myself, "Don't stop believing you can do this." When my parents tell this story, it sounds like I was having a deep, spiritual moment, but in truth I was joking around, trying to swim to my mom and wondering how far I could go.

When I got to what felt like the middle of the lake, I floated on my back, spreading out my arms and legs like a starfish, looking up at the blue sky. I was alone, truly alone. Nobody watching would have noticed me and thought, "Hey, that kid is alone." After all, there were plenty of other people in the lake, and I knew three of them. My mother was on a paddleboard. My brother and father were somewhere behind me. But, as far as I was concerned, I was alone and that was not an ordinary day.

We've gone swimming as a family plenty of times. My dad used to be a lifeguard, so he loves to swim. I've watched him throw my brother, Jacob, in various pools and bodies of water for as long as I can remember. And countless times Jacob has cannon-balled into the water right near me just to irritate my mother. Whenever we went to a pool or a lake, my mother, who never really learned to swim right, hov-ered near me in the shallow end, keeping the coast clear of splashy toddlers and annoying younger brothers. And every single time I went swimming, up until this day, I had to wear water wings on my hands and feet and a life preserver around my stom-ach to keep my head as far above the water as pos-sible. Even to doggy paddle would have put my neck dangerously close to the surface of the water. Water, in this situation, was my kryptonite.

But on this day, for the first time ever, the embar-rassing water wings were gone. My mother was giving me space. For a good distance, all around me, there was only water. It was amazing and ordinary at the same time.

I was thirteen years old, and I had never been able to swim by myself. I had put my head under water a few times, just for a few seconds, but that was completely against the doctors' orders. Now, sixty-seven surgeries later, I could finally swim like normal kids, without numerous flotation devices bobbling around me, without an adult ready to help me if something went wrong.

If you looked at it from the outside, I had worked really hard for this moment—having operations to help me breathe, recovering from the surgery, getting used to a new normal, then doing the whole thing all over again many times—but surgeries didn't feel like something I deserved applause for achieving. I'd been having surgeries ever since I was born. What I felt in Beaver Lake wasn't a sense of accomplishment. It felt more like, after wanting to do something for a long while, I'd finally been allowed to do it without my parents for the first time. A ride on the school bus. A sleepover. What I imagine it will feel like when I can finally drive a car. I'd wanted to swim by myself for so long, it was hard to believe it was actually real. My brain was still processing the change. But the water was energizing. The sky was wide open. The whole world stretched around me. I felt free.

PART I

A BEAUTIFUL
BABY BOY

Draconian Does Not Mean Fun

NATHANIEL About a year and a half before I went swimming in Beaver Lake, when I was eleven, my parents had taken me to meet with a new doctor at Seattle Children's Hospital. Another doctor's appointment, woo-hoo. But my parents were very excited to hear about a new surgery this guy, Dr. Hopper, was doing.

Starting before I was born, my face didn't form properly, so doctors had been trying to help me function for my entire life. I could hardly breathe. My nose didn't connect to my airway, and because my jaw was so small, my tongue filled my mouth. There were problems with most of my senses. I couldn't smell or breathe because extra bones were behind my nose, blocking it. I couldn't eat because my jaw was small and out of alignment. I could barely hear because I didn't have ears to capture the sound and deliver it to my brain. I didn't have bottom eyelids, which meant I couldn't close my eyes fully, and my vision wasn't great, although that was just run-of-the-mill bad luck. Bonus! The only good news on my five senses report card was that I could touch—everything about me from the neck down worked just fine. And my brain was perfectly fine too, maybe even a little bit awesome, if I do say so myself, which would help me deal with all the other problems.

I grew up knowing that I was born with a syndrome called Treacher Collins and that it made me different, but I didn't feel different. I felt like myself, the only self I'd ever known. Other kids weren't fed through a tube in their stomach for the first year and a half of their lives. Other kids didn't wear hearing aids. Other kids didn't have a hole in their neck to help them to breathe. Other kids didn't grow up having doctors' appointments instead of soccer practice and surgeries instead of vacations. Other kids didn't have a nurse with them at school. Other kids could shower, swim, play roughly, go out in the rain. But the way I see it, a certain number of kids are going to be born with issues like mine every year. One in forty thousand to one in seventy thousand, if you ask the people who count up these things. That's not very many, but that's just kids with Treacher Collins. Tens of thousands of kids are born with facial differences in North America every year. Plenty more kids have different problems to deal with. I'm definitely not going to do the math on that, but I know that if you add all those kids together, I'm just one in a huge crowd. If you look at it that way, I'm pretty normal after all.

MAGDA   For our first appointment, Nathaniel's dad, Russel, and I, Nathaniel's mom, sat down in chairs in front of Dr. Hopper's desk. Nathaniel picked a bench off to the side of the room. Dr. Hopper was pioneering a new surgery. He hoped to dramatically change Nathaniel's ability to breathe, at last setting him free from the tubes and pumps and antibiotics that had entangled him for his whole life.

The very first thing Dr. Hopper said to the three of us was, "You'll hate what I'm going to tell you. It's draconian." I explained to Nathaniel that *draconian* meant extremely harsh. He registered that, then went back to drawing on a piece of paper the nurse had given him.

Dr. Hopper went on to explain that if we agreed to the surgery, he and his team would try to change the structure of Nathaniel's entire face. It would take several preparatory surgeries, and then the biggest one would be a whopper, not just because of the eleven-hour procedure itself, but because of what came afterward. The follow-up treatment was not very different from what you might invent to torture your worst enemy. (Sure, when you torture your worst enemy, the end goal usually isn't to give the guy a chance to breathe through his nose and without the help of a trach, but otherwise this was exactly the same.) For now, I'll just say that it involved four months of wearing a heavy cage around his head, attached by screws.

In the end, if the surgery was successful, it would change Nathaniel's life. He would still look like himself, the doctor promised us, but for the first time since he was six weeks old, he wouldn't need a breathing tube. He would be able to take a shower, and yes, he'd be allowed to swim.

Dr. Hopper said, "The entire process, including six surgeries, will take a year to a year and a half, but it might work." Nathaniel would only be the third child to have the procedure. It was as if the doctors, amongst themselves, had said, "If we can fix Nathaniel Newman, we can fix anyone."

The description of the treatment was not a pleasant thing for a parent to hear. I wondered how it was sounding to the eleven-year-old would-be patient. "You're doing this because we said so" wouldn't fly in this case. It was torture! He couldn't wake up surprised to find his head in a vise. We had to make sure he knew what he was getting himself into, and he had to be on board. That was why we'd brought Nathaniel with us to Dr. Hopper's office to hear everything he had to say.

When the doctor finished describing this terrible but potentially miraculous plan, his dad and I looked at our son to see his reaction. Nathaniel was in the corner of the room. He had a sheet of white paper taped to his chest. He'd colored the paper red, and there were big holes stabbed through it, as if he'd been riddled with bullets.

"What are you doing?" we asked him.

I think we both expected him to say: "This is what you want to do to me. You're going to destroy me."

Instead, he cheerfully said, "You're not going to believe it. We've been overrun by monkeys, and they all have muskets."

Nathaniel had always found his way through the pain and suffering, and this was exactly how he did it. Monkeys and muskets one day, a team of superheroes another—these characters and their comic book battles distracted him from bad news, boredom, and pain.

Russel pressed him. "Nathaniel, this is serious. It's going to suck. Did you hear the details? Do you have any questions? What do you think?"

Nathaniel looked up. He asked, "Do I get to miss school?"

Russel said, "Yes, you will miss three months of school."

Nathaniel gave a double thumbs-up. "Awesome. Let's do it."

NATHANIEL   I was bored. To be honest, I'm always bored when doctors are talking, but my parents make me turn off my iPad when there's "stuff I need to hear." So I had asked a nurse for a marker. The one she gave me happened to be red. While I "listened," I drew a bullet hole on a piece of paper and taped it to myself. Did it mean I had a death wish? No! Occasionally, I draw laser beams going through people. This doesn't mean I'm violent or insane. It just means I like the way I draw laser beams.

Ever since I could remember, I'd had a tracheostomy to help me breathe. Without it, I wouldn't be alive today. A trach is a tube that looks like a mini-drinking straw. It goes from a button-like valve on your neck to your windpipe (on the inside, of course) to help you breathe if you can't do it independently. For my whole life I'd known my life-saving trach was (a) a danger to my health and (b) a huge inconvenience. But it was also all I'd ever known. It felt normal to me.

Imagine if someone came up to you and said, "Wow, you have to go to the bathroom several times a day? Your body doesn't just take care of that on its own? I feel so sorry for you. That must be gross and annoying." And you looked around and noticed that nobody else had to interrupt what they were doing to take a bathroom break. You were the only one. Nobody else even had bathrooms in their houses, so you had to carry around special equipment to handle your unusual needs.

Then you might say, "Okay, I get it. Their bodies work better than mine." You would understand that idea, but it would still be hard to actually know what it felt like for your body to work just like theirs, what it felt like to be "normal."

When I said, "Awesome! Let's do it!" to Dr. Hopper, I was acting like the surgery was no big deal, but I really did like the possibility of being able to swim farther, deeper, for longer, without an adult hovering nearby. And though it was hard for me to imagine, I knew that if I didn't have a trach, so many of the medical issues I dealt with every day would just . . . disappear. I wouldn't get infections. I wouldn't worry about someone bumping into the trach. My parents wouldn't have to change the trach tie (which held it in place). I wouldn't have to get a new trach every two weeks. The cap wouldn't pop out and fly down the school hallway when I sneezed, as it once had done in front of my entire class. I was used to having the trach be part of my life, but it wasn't too hard to conclude, based on observation, that life without it would be a whole lot easier. I liked what the surgery promised, and I wanted to have it and for it to be successful, but I didn't want to get my hopes up.

MAGDA From the day he was born, Nathaniel accepted his physical challenges, but people around him had a little more trouble. He looked different to them. He didn't look "normal." People had strange, awkward, sometimes mean responses to seeing him.

Normal. When you take what is most common and call it normal, you are suggesting that there is something abnormal, something wrong, something *bad*, about not being like most other people. There is judgement in the word. When I yearned for normal, I wanted Nathaniel to have the comfort and opportunities that any other kid would take for granted. I also wanted him to be free from that judgment.

Normal was our goal, but for us *normal* meant seeing, eating, hearing, breathing. Normal was a happy, carefree childhood.

Surprise!

NATHANIEL Parents sometimes tell their kids the story of how they were born: "Johnny was born with a full head of hair, just like his father!" or "Oh you had the tiniest, most perfect hands," or "You slept through the night from the day you were born." The story my parents told went a little deeper, and they didn't make up a happy, fairy-tale version of it.

My parents were normal (whatever that means) married people, and when I came into the world it was rather shocking. When my mother got pregnant, they moved from Manhattan across the river to Hoboken, New Jersey, where they could afford a bigger apartment. My mom was writing a major paper to finish up grad school for music. She'd been studying at a music academy in Gdańsk, Poland, where she was born. My dad was starting a new career at an insurance company. He wanted to impress my mother and convince her she'd made the right choice to leave her life in Poland for him.

My parents had only been married for a year, but they were excited to have a baby, and they expected it to be something of a surprise. I mean, every baby is a surprise to their parents in some way. Maybe they don't know if it's going to be a boy or a girl, or maybe the kid has unexpected red hair. But I was a completely different story.

In the hospital room, when I was born, my mom thought that she would hear the cry of a newborn. Instead, the way she tells it, everyone in the room went silent. The doctor and nurses looked completely freaked out. They bundled me up and hurried me off to a side room. My father followed them.

"What's going on?" my mom asked. "Where's my baby?"

And then she heard my dad crying, but she still wasn't hearing a peep from me.

"Is the baby alive?" my mom asked.

Nobody answered.

My mom looked over to the side room, where she caught her first glimpse of me. She saw the side of my head, where my ear should have been, but it didn't look like a normal ear. Her first thought was, *I'm a musician! How can I have a baby who can't hear?*

Then she saw my profile. The ear was just the beginning. Something was very wrong with me.

My mom doesn't sugarcoat the story of my birth. She gives it to me straight. After she caught that first glimpse of me she asked the doctor, "Did I deliver an alien?"

Yeah. My mother. The one person who is supposed lay on the love a little too thick from day one. My own mother thought I was an alien. Nice.

Don't get me wrong. Being from another planet would be cool. And it would mean there was somewhere in the world where my body worked and made sense. Unfortunately, I was stuck on Earth.

I think of my mom as very tough, but she can also get hysterical. Not hysterical-funny. More like hysterical-crazy. It took her a while to process the surprise of this very different-looking baby. She was in her hospital room, recovering from my birth—she still hadn't held me or even gotten a close look at me.

My dad came back from the nursery. "We don't know what's wrong, but the baby's face is severely deformed," he told her. Some people with facial differences don't like the word *deformed*. I was just a baby, so I had no opinion on the matter, but even now I don't mind it. It's definitely less offensive than *alien*. Mostly people prefer to use *facial difference*, so I try to do that, and now my dad does too.

Finally, some doctors came into the room and gave my parents a book, open to a picture of a person with droopy eyes and a really small jaw.

"Your son has Treacher Collins syndrome. It's a congenital disorder (*congenital* means something a person is born with). His ears, eyes, cheekbones, jaw-bone—they haven't formed normally," said one of the doctors.

My mom was in shock.

Another doctor added, "He will be physically challenged. He has almost no jaw. He can't hear. He's having trouble breathing."

The next day, while my parents were processing this upsetting news, some of my relatives on my dad's side started to gather in the hospital room, but nobody was celebrating, like they usually do when a baby is born. Instead people were crying as if someone had died. I wasn't dead! I was very much alive, with lots of PlayStation in my future, but nobody had gotten used to that idea. My mom was overloaded with worry and fear. Like I said, hysterical-crazy.

MÁGDA I know the story I'm supposed to tell Nathaniel about his birth. "You were our perfect little angel, a gift from God." But we have always been truthful with Nathaniel, even when it comes to our own doubts and fears and failures. If we made his story all shiny and perfect, well, we wouldn't be us and he wouldn't be him. The truth is that I was scared and had no idea how Nathaniel could live with all these complications. How could I take care of him? Why was this happening to us? Was God punishing us? Could I love this child? These were big questions, and I couldn't just solve them by googling "will my baby be okay?" on my phone. I was afraid to hold him or even look at him before I'd answered them.

That night, after Russel's family went home, I lay in the hospital bed and prayed. *This is the worst day of my life. Give me strength. Give me a sign. Give me something to hold on to.*

It was February 8, 2004. Nathaniel was less than a day old. The TV was playing in the recovery room, and the Grammys were on. Christina Aguilera came onscreen. The singer walked onto an empty, round platform, dressed simply in a dark suit, with bare feet and dark hair. She began to sing her hit song, "You are beautiful no matter what they say, words can't bring you down."

It's a beautiful, moving song, and it stopped us in our tracks. Russel and I stared at each other in absolute amazement. It was like Christina Aguilera was speaking directly to us. Her words didn't solve any of Nathaniel's medical issues, but they answered all the questions and fears that were circling in my head. Something changed in that moment. A weird, new feeling of strength rose in me. I don't usually believe in this kind of thing, but it felt like I'd asked God for a sign and he'd given me one. No matter how my child looked, he was going to be beautiful. I had been chosen to be his mother. I would love him. I already did. I always had.

Russel was holding my hand. Right then, as we listened to the song, I promised God that I would do everything I possibly could to raise our child as a beautiful soul, a beautiful spirit, a beautiful human.

We both cried, but I had different tears now. These weren't tears of fear but tears of possibility. I was going to turn this situation around and make the best possible outcome.

Russel said, "Magda, this is going to be our beautiful child no matter what happens. He's going to change the world one day." Every parent wants their newborn child to change the world, right? Well, Russel and I had the same hope, it was just that before Nathaniel got started making the world a better place, we needed him to live.

We walked to the nursery where our baby was resting. I was ready to meet him. My destiny was to raise a child who was born deaf, unable to eat or close his eyes, barely able to breathe. A world where the most basic functions are hard-won victories.

A world where only science and love make anything possible.

NATHANIEL Well, my parents may have needed to hear a Christina Aguilera song to pull themselves together, but they soon came around to the idea of me. I get it. When my little brother Jacob came home from the hospital, I had to come around to the idea of him, and he didn't even have various medical tubes sprouting from his body. Besides, once my parents decided they could handle me, they became like most parents: they helped me walk; they taught me my ABCs; they wanted me to say "please" and make friends and do well in school. They expected me to be kind to my little brother (even when whatever went wrong was his fault). All that same old stuff, it's just that on top was a pretty important extra layer: keeping me alive.

Gift from God

MÁGDA We named our son Nathaniel. Later, when it came time to pick a Hebrew name for him, our rabbi said, "You don't have to choose a different name. Nathaniel is already a Hebrew name. It means 'gift from God.'"

It would be a while before I reached into the pocket of an old coat and found a little notebook that I had once used for addresses, train schedules, recipes, and odd notes. Written in it was a list of baby names that Russel and I had come up with several years before, when we first met. Sitting at a cafe in Prague, we talked about having kids one day, and we scrawled out a few names. For a boy, we had written down Nathaniel and Jakub (the Polish form of Jacob). Long before our special boy was born, we had somehow anticipated our gift from God.

That same day, back in Prague, the question of religion came up. In the town where I grew up there were more churches than supermarkets. My parents were devout Catholics, and we went to church every Sunday morning. If I wanted to sleep in (which I always did), I'd go to mass by myself in the afternoon. To be honest, when I was a kid I wasn't the biggest fan of church. As a teenager, I'd bring a portable CD player (what us old folks had before iPods) and hide in the back of the church where the organ-player was. During the mass, while the priest rambled on about topics that didn't seem relevant to my life, I'd listen to music. But I believed in God and spoke to him often, and even if I wasn't a model attendee, I liked the commitment and ritual of going to church.

I had grown up in this very religious household and community. Russel had grown up in a not-as-religious Jewish family.

When we talked about our future family, I said, "I know so much about Catholicism, and it was a big part of my life growing up. I'd like our kids to be Catholic."

Russel said, "I want them to learn about Judaism too."

"But you didn't practice religion as much as I did," I said. "Your parents didn't go to temple every week the way I went to church."

But Russel said his Jewish identity was part of his daily life.

I suggested a compromise. "We both believe in one god, we just acknowledge it differently. So let's have God decide. If our first child is a boy, because you're a man, let's raise him and the rest of our children Jewish. I'll do everything in my power to learn about your religion and to raise our children to follow it. And if God gives us a daughter first, that means he decided we should raise all our kids Catholic."

It was a little unorthodox, so to speak, but Russel liked this idea. "Okay," he agreed. "We'll have God decide."

When we found out we were having a boy, I was in shock for a couple of days. I would be leaving my religion behind. My children wouldn't go to church. My family and hometown would not know what to think. But I still believed that most religions come back to one god, with different ways of showing devotion to that god.

In Poland we say: "The world is a theater. God is a director. You are an actor." It's okay that I don't know in advance what the play is about. God is directing me. Anyway, if God is the director, he cast my children as Jews. So we joined a temple in Hoboken and went to couples' classes on Judaism twice a week until Nathaniel was born. Russel and I attended those classes for fun and enlightenment, oblivious to how soon we would be at God's doorstep, questioning him and asking for guidance.

Burrito

NATHANIEL My mom describes the moment in the hospital when she went to meet me for the first time as feeling like she was stepping on stage to give a speech or about to take a test. This only makes sense if you know that when my mom was growing up she was a star pianist. It was a big part of her life. She performed in concerts and piano competitions all the time, so she knew how to take a deep breath and do her best no matter how nervous she was.

MÁGDA When I walked into the nursery in the NICU (neonatal intensive care unit) to meet Nathaniel, the first thing I saw were Nathaniel's long legs, poking out over the end of the bassinet, which had been designed for tiny babies who were born prematurely. Then I saw his little face with big, big eyes. He was gasping for air. He was almost a day old and he still hadn't had anything to eat yet because he couldn't suck. But somehow, inconceivably, he seemed to be smiling at me. I held him in my arms and said, "I love you. I love you," half to reassure myself that I did love him. Then I looked him in the eyes, saw the tiny human in there, wanting to survive, wanting to live. My baby. Gazing at him, I thought, *You're my soulmate now. I'm going to protect you and make sure you're okay. I'll provide anything you need.*

The hospital staff were getting nervous about the fact that this baby hadn't had anything to eat. He couldn't nurse. He couldn't take a bottle. He choked on formula from a syringe. He had the instinct to suck— he'd try, making little sucking noises, but physically he just couldn't do it. His jaw was so tiny that his tongue, which was normal-size, was too big for the space it had. He would cough as he tried to breathe and swallow at the same time.

The hospital where Nathaniel was born didn't have anyone specializing in Treacher Collins. So the next morning the nurses wrapped Nathaniel up like a burrito and we all headed across town to NYU Langone

Medical Center. In the ambulance, I watched every breath he took.

As soon as we brought our day-old son into the craniofacial ward at NYU, a woman greeted us at the door and introduced herself as Shelley Cohen. Shelley had arranged for the transfer to this hospital and had been waiting for us to arrive.

She came up to me, smiled into the bundle I was carrying, and said, "Congratulations, you have a beautiful baby boy."

It was the first time anyone had congratulated me on the birth of my son! When Shelley treated me and Nathaniel like any other mother and baby, her kind words gave me hope that they would come true. That he would one day be able to function like most babies. That there was a way for us to come closer to normal, to climb out of this nightmare into being parents and child, in a home not a hospital, eating meals as a family. What had seemed like a given was now just a dream.

NATHANIEL In my first two days at NYU Langone Medical Center, I had my first two surgeries. My parents had no idea that it was just the beginning and that by age thirteen I would have had more than sixty surgeries and counting! But my mom reminds me that surgery is always a big deal, especially when you're little and fragile.

The first surgery was to put in a gastrointestinal tube. This "g-tube" was so that I could be fed directly through a tube to my stomach until the doctors figured out how I could use my mouth. My parents hoped this was a temporary solution, but nobody knew for sure.

The second thing the doctors did was to drill a hole in the bone that was blocking my nose. I was only breathing through my tiny mouth. This surgery was supposed to help me breathe through my nose, but nobody knew if it would work.

When they stabilized me at NYU, it helped my mom calm down.

MAGDA We had a long and bumpy road ahead, but behind Nathaniel's face, which cried out for help and repair, I saw a curious little mind, ready to greet the world. My child would learn about butterflies, get lost in books, and explore the world, even if often from a hospital bed. He was so much more than a baby who needed help.

NATHANIEL My dad tells me, "The picture I have in my mind is your mother, sitting in a rocking chair in the hospital. She is clutching you to her chest. Tubes are springing out of you in every direction, but your mom is humming, caressing you, loving you."

MAGDA Nathaniel was already a month old when we finally brought him home from the hospital. Our little apartment in Hoboken was only two rooms, so Nathaniel's crib was in our bedroom. We had picked a set of Winnie-the-Pooh crib sheets, and with them came a couple of pictures of Winnie-the-Pooh that I'd hung on the wall next to the crib. I'd carefully organized his clothes in a dresser that had a changing station on top. It had only been a couple of months earlier when we were preparing for his arrival, but it already felt like a lifetime ago.

I rested him in the crib, though there had been a few adjustments to the sweet, calm nest where I'd envisioned nursing him and singing lullabies. It was surrounded with equipment, like a hospital room. There were tall poles from which the feeding bags hung, and boxes of extra bags and baby formula.

Nathaniel had already outgrown most of those newborn clothes, and he couldn't wear the ones that might have fit. I cleared them out to make room for clothes with buttons in the front so we could access the g-tube when we wanted to feed him.

Bringing a new baby home is always an adjustment. Taking care of this baby was a little more complicated than burping and the occasional diaper blowout. Nathaniel's g-tube looked like an extra belly button, and it was the only way he could eat. But he had trouble keeping formula down, "trouble" being an understatement. Pretty much as soon as we got home, Nathaniel started throwing up the formula. All of it. In it went, out it came. Backwards. Because instead of in through the mouth, down to the stomach, it was in through the stomach, up to the mouth. He threw up as I fed him.

I dragged our ruined carpets out to the curb, resterilized the equipment, and tried again. I measured ingredients, tested different brands and products, but nothing worked. The doctors told me to set the feeding pump on drip and to feed him all night long so he'd get extra food while he slept. If he wriggled at all, the tube would pop out and the pump would be feeding the bed instead of Nathaniel. I half-slept, keeping guard. I wanted to give him the baby's life that seemed normal to me, but I was slow-drip feeding him for hours at a time, only to watch him throw it all back up. Additionally, babies are supposed to have "tummy time," to strengthen their spines, but Nathaniel's g-tube made it very uncomfortable for him. I piled tons of blankets on the floor to cushion the tube and tried to entertain him with books and toys.

To Breathe

NATHANIEL Two weeks after we got home from the hospital, when I was six weeks old, we went to Long Island for the weekend to visit my grandparents. My uncles lived nearby with their families, and now that I had finally left the hospital, they wanted all of my cousins—who hadn't been allowed in the NICU— to have their first chance to meet me. I'm sure that if I'd been able to speak at that young age, my first words would have been, "Do you have any dogs, and if so, can you please put me down in sight of them?" (I love dogs.) Unfortunately, I was only a loveable but word-less blob, as babies are. My grandmother made pot roast, her favorite family meal, and everyone passed me around. A run-of-the-mill meet-the-newborn family weekend. Except . . .

Over the course of a day—that one day at his grandparents' house!—Nathaniel's breathing changed. He was sleeping next to me in a portable crib, and at one in the morning I woke up to hear him making a terrible snoring noise. Looking over, I saw that his chest was rising and falling too heavily. He was gasping for breath. I shook Russel awake.

"Something's not right."

We turned on the light. Nathaniel was turning blue. Russel got the doctor on the phone.

"This doesn't sound good," Dr. Bernstein said. "You need to come to the hospital as soon as possible."

One of the first two surgeries had helped Nathaniel to breathe on his own. The doctors had warned us that this might not last—he might need a breathing tube at some point—but we had been hoping to spare him from it. Now, as we loaded ourselves into the car, Dr. Bernstein explained that over the past two weeks Nathaniel's tongue had probably grown, but his jaw hadn't, so now it had reached a point where his tongue was too big for his mouth, which was making it difficult for him to get enough air. At the same time, the passage they'd made behind his nose was starting to close up. So he'd gone from breathing through both his nose and his mouth to having trouble breathing through either.

Dr. Bernstein told us to keep him face-down as we drove so his tongue would drop away from his throat, giving a bit more room for air to pass through.

It was at least an hour from Russel's parents' house to the hospital. Russel drove, and I sat in the back seat with Nathaniel between my legs, his head facing the floor through my knees. So much for using a car seat. Breathing takes priority over being buckled up for safety.

Russel drove as fast as he could on the icy roads, and we were lucky it was the middle of the night, because at one point he lost control and we started spinning in circles in the middle of the highway. I was screaming. Russel was screaming. The doctor, who was still on the phone, must have thought Long Island was going down in flames. When we skidded to a stop, there was a moment of silence, then we heard him say, "How's it going there, guys?"

An army of doctors met us in the ER. Nathaniel was given an emergency tracheotomy.

Now, when you looked at Nathaniel, you saw a band around his neck (the trach tie), with a button in the front (a valve that let air in, or a cap). The trach was not just a temporary emergency fix. The only way he would ever be able to get rid of it would be if doctors could some-day re-open the bone behind his nose so that he had an airway again. It didn't sound too bad—they'd done that once already, right? But that bone, which had been soft and easy to open when he was a newborn, would harden and thicken and cause us no end of trouble.

When Nathaniel woke up from the tracheotomy, his voice was gone. He wasn't used to the tube that now ran alongside his vocal cords. Until he was big enough and strong enough to use a special cap for the trach, he wouldn't be able to make a noise. The only way I could tell when he was crying was that his mouth would be wide open, his face turning purple. A screaming baby with no voice. If you've ever hung out around a scream-ing baby, you might think this was an improvement, but to me, his mother, it was heartbreaking.

The new, life-saving trach was not an easy fix. It lim-ited his activities and required a lot of attention. It's hard to live a normal life with a trach. You don't see a lot of people walking around with trachs. You don't see doc-tors with trachs—no teachers, no waiters, no judges, not many people out there in the world, leading so-called normal lives and having normal careers, with a trach.

When you understand the challenges of having a trach, then you can easily see why we didn't spend any time worrying about what Nathaniel looked like. Soon after he was born, after spending only a few hours with him, he just looked like himself to us, our sweet baby. The trach was what prevented him from being a healthy, carefree kid.

Our overall goal immediately became to get rid of it one day, the sooner the better. The longer you keep a trach in, the longer you are dependent on it, the more likely it is that you will have it for the rest of your life. Your body and brain get used to it. When I dreamed of "normal" for Nathaniel, my biggest dream became to free him from needing the trach to breathe.

NATHANIEL The trach saved my life, but it was a beast. It had to be kept really clean, and it had to be clear so that I could breathe through it. What might clog it up, you wonder? Boogers. There are way more boogers than you think, boogers that you swallow all day long without ever seeing them. I'm sorry but it's true. And mine couldn't be swallowed. They needed to be cleared out of my trach frequently using a suction machine that sucked my boogers out through a hose and into a canister. Don't be jealous. Day and night, no matter what was going on, my parents always listened to my breath. When it sounded rough, like there was mucus stuck in my throat, they suctioned me. They always did it to me while I slept, and I'm pretty sure they were half-asleep a lot of the time. My mom tells me there were lots of instances when I pushed her hand away, saying, "Leave me alone." That might sound kind of rude, but I don't think people who don't get suctioned in the middle of the night get to decide what counts as rude.

When the weather was good and I was perfectly healthy my mom might only have to suction my trach maybe ten times a day. But when I was sick, she sometimes did it seventy times in a single day. The suctioning was a constant interruption, though I was used to it and needed it, otherwise it would start to feel like I couldn't get enough air, kind of like the feeling when you have to cough.

The hardest part of having the trach was that no water could get in it. Think about that for a second. No water allowed to touch your neck. Ever. My mom tells me that I loved getting in a little blue bathtub that sat on top of the sink, but I wasn't allowed to get wet from the neck up. To wash my head, my mom used a damp baby washcloth with a tiny bit of baby soap. If water found its way around the trach tie and into my lungs, it was a bad scene. Basically, I would drown.

My mom had the suction machine next to the bathtub at all times.

So the trach was important, but it also sucked. No pun intended.

MAGDA Having a trach comes with a whole package of maintenance. Carrying a suction machine at all times. Keeping the trach clean. Changing it regularly at the doctor's office. Having a hole in your neck with a tube that your body is constantly trying to reject and repair is an ongoing battle. The trach was prone to infections. Or, rather, infections flocked to it like ants to a sugar cube. We went to the doctor to get a clean, new one every two weeks, and Nathaniel had to be on antibiotics practically all winter long.

Once, early on, Nathaniel got a trach infection. I suctioned him forty times in one day and saw that soon I was going to run out of a medical device called a suction catheter. The suction catheter looks like a small tube—we had many small tubes in different sizes in our supplies closet. (They would have been kind of fun to play with if they hadn't been so crucial to Nathaniel's survival.) If I ran out of new catheters, I couldn't suction Nathaniel, and if I didn't suction him, he would not be able to breathe. But this was a weekend, and we couldn't just walk into a drugstore to pick up more catheters. They're not as common as Band-Aids. In a panic, I called a new friend, Jenna (not her real name), a mom I'd met who also had a child with Treacher Collins.

Jenna's daughter, Emily, was two years older than Nathaniel. I asked Jenna if she had any catheters left over from when Emily had a trach. It turned out she did have a box sitting in her basement. Even though it was the middle of the night, Russel drove over to her Brooklyn townhouse—about an hour away—to pick them up.

When Russel got home two hours later, he dropped the box of catheters on the kitchen counter and went to the bedroom to crash. He only had a couple of hours to sleep before he left for Long Island. His brother, Hal, was turning his basement into an apartment, and Russel had promised to spend the day helping. I stayed home with Nathaniel.

The catheters from Jenna were in a box that looked exactly like the ones mine came in. It was still sealed from the factory. Later that morning, when I ran out of catheters, I used a knife to slice through the sealing tape. When I innocently pulled up the first flap, hundreds of cockroaches flew out at me. My hand was instantly black with them. I screamed! It was like a horror movie. I freaked out, waving my arms wildly to fling the roaches away. I grabbed Nathaniel, the bag with the pump in it, and my phone—the person and things I could not live without—and escaped from the apartment. I called Russel from the hallway.

"They're everywhere!" I screamed into the phone. "Oh my God! Help!" Russel thought I was being murdered. It took a solid minute of screaming before I managed to communicate to him that I was living my worst nightmare.

"Okay, Magda. Go back in. Grab your wallet and keys. Make sure you have everything, then leave the apartment. Close the door."

By the time I summoned enough courage to fetch my wallet and keys, the roaches had formed a long line, hundreds of them marching down the kitchen counter and across the floor. They looked like they had a plan. My feeling was, if they wanted this apartment, they could have it. We couldn't afford the rent anyway.

Out in the hallway, I broke the doctor's rules. I was supposed to use a new catheter every time, but I decided that battling cockroaches for ownership of a new catheter was worse than a dirty catheter. So I cleaned a used catheter as best I could and suctioned Nathaniel.

Russel ditched the work he was doing on his brother's basement and came all the way back home to help me. We packed up our bags and supplies and headed to Russel's parents' house on Long Island. From the car, we called Pat Chibbaro at NYU. Nurse Pat was one of our favorite nurses at NYU Langone Medical Center who had become a friend.

We begged her for extra catheters to get us through the weekend, then drove over to the hospital to pick them up. It wouldn't be the only time we turned to our medical family at NYU for emergency supplies.

Then we called an exterminator and scheduled him to bomb the apartment.

NATHANIEL I am not a fan of cockroaches. Maybe this story explains why. If I had to face an army of cockroaches, I would run for my life. But my dogs would probably fight over who could eat the most. That might be worth watching. From a good distance.

Soup

MAGDA We thought our biggest challenge was taking care of Nathaniel's medical needs, but sometimes life is like a block tower—pull out one block and the rest comes tumbling down. Money was immediately a problem. As hard as Russel was working—he received two promotions in the first two years of Nathaniel's life—most of the doctors at NYU didn't take insurance. The bills poured in. It might be $35,000 for one surgery. If Nathaniel had three procedures in one fell swoop, it could easily cost $100,000. Health insurance covered some of it, and an organization called the National Foundation for Facial Reconstruction (now called myFace) often paid the rest, but somehow there were always more bills. A lot of the time we were supposed to pay the bills ourselves, then wait for insurance to reimburse us. If it took too long to receive their checks, we ran out of money. One day I was at the grocery store with a cart full of food, and when I tried to pay, my debit card was denied. Our bank account was frozen. I had to go back to our apartment with no groceries.

NATHANIEL My mother grew up on an organic farm in Poland, and her childhood was really different from mine. I know this because she likes nothing more than to tell me about it. I haven't been to Poland yet, but I've heard all of her stories about it, most of them lots of times, but I don't mind. It helped me understand, from the time I was really little, that there are many different ways to experience the world. I had my experience, she had hers, and all over the world children are having their own. There is no one way that is the right or normal way to grow up. When she tells me these stories, it's like I flash back in time.

ZAP! FLASHBACK!

MAGDA Our farm was in Sanok, a village in the Carpathian Mountains of Poland, close to the

Ukraine border. At mealtime, my siblings and I ate whatever my mother gave us. There was no such thing as pickiness. We ate or we went hungry.

All winter long my mother made soups. One room in our basement had a dark, wet, flat mud floor. That's where she kept root vegetables in the winter—piles of potatoes, carrots, and parsley root. Another basement room had shelves and a high window where we stored jars of pickles, tomatoes, mushrooms, compote, jams, and jellies. All this food was harvested from our farm and pickled and canned by my mother. The basement hasn't changed at all since I was young, though of course the food stored there gets replaced every year.

NATHANIEL My mom says that if you can find the time, you can always make soup. The base is always the same: onions, garlic, chicken stock, and whatever vegetables you have on hand. She says that if you know how to make soup, you'll always have a meal, because soup can be made from whatever is around. That is my mother's homespun wisdom in a nutshell. *There's always a soup to be made* is her way of telling me to make the best of every situation.

MÁGDA When my debit card was rejected, I left the grocery store empty-handed. I thought, *There's always a soup to be made.* All we had at home was rice and apples. I remembered that when I was little and food was in short supply, my grandma used to make a meal out of rice baked with apples, cinnamon, and sugar. So that was what Russel and I ate until Russel straightened out the debit card situation. I knew if my mother and grandmother could make it work, so would I.

We needed to catch up with our medical bills—we could no longer afford to pay our rent in Hoboken. Luckily, Russel's brother, Hal, and his wife, Nancy, generously offered to build an apartment in their basement for us. This was the basement that Russel had been helping to fix up when I was attacked by killer cockroaches.

Hal and Nancy lived in Wading River, on Long Island's North Fork, in a two-story house. Hal had divided the basement space into a living room, bedroom, kitchenette, and bathroom. He added wall-to-wall carpeting and finished the walls, doing his best to make it welcoming for us. We moved to the basement apartment when Nathaniel was almost six months old.

Nathaniel's first craniofacial surgeon at NYU, Dr. Joseph McCarthy, gave me the right advice at the right time. Even though his goal as a doctor was to improve Nathaniel's life from a medical perspective, Dr. McCarthy made sure to tell us that we should give him a real childhood despite the challenges brought on by Treacher Collins. "We can fix a broken bone if he falls on the playground," said Dr. McCarthy, "but if you don't let him have a normal childhood we won't be able to fix his psyche."

Nathaniel needed to be suctioned frequently and fed for hours a day, but I still did my best to play and walk and read with him the way most mothers do.

NATHANIEL When we moved to my aunt and uncle's basement, my dad needed our only car to get to work, but my mom found any way she could to take me out in nature. Most days we would walk to the grocery store, which doesn't sound very exciting to me, especially when there's no junk food involved, but I guess it's entertaining enough for a baby in a stroller. The store was right down the highway, but there was no sidewalk, so my mom found a shortcut through someone's field. Later, in the winter, she remembers pushing the stroller across that long stretch of frozen grass, leaving stroller marks across the fresh snow.

On weekends, she and my dad took me to the beach, even though the wind blew sand into my trach, because they wanted me to see and smell the ocean as best I could.

My mom had a rental piano which she paid for by teaching a few piano students. She sat me on her lap and played piano for me—I couldn't hear well, but she played loudly so I could feel the vibrations.

Sometimes she would turn on classical music, blocking her ears to match her hearing to mine, then turning up the volume until she thought it was loud enough for me. She sang loudly, right near my nonexistent ears. I was still too young to respond, but since she was a musician, raising me with music was really important to my mom, so she hoped it was coming through.

Some parents might tell their kids cute stories from their childhood about what their first words were, or how they climbed out of their crib. My mom tells me the story of the first time my trach fell out. We'd only been in the basement apartment for a few weeks when my mom checked on me in the middle of the night and realized that my trach had somehow popped out. This was a bad thing.

As soon as the trach came out, the hole would start to close, so it was a race against the clock to put it back in place. The doctors had told my parents that if it ever came out, they had maybe fifteen minutes to put it back. If they failed, I would need surgery. My parents didn't know if I could breathe long enough to survive the trip to the hospital.

MÁGDA The doctors had explained to us how to replace the tube in an emergency, but neither Russel nor I had ever actually done it. This was a perfect example of how, even though we were the parents, we had no idea what we were doing.

We brought Nathaniel upstairs and put him on the kitchen table where there was an overhead light. Russel tried to replace the trach, but the hole in Nathaniel's neck started bleeding. I hovered over the baby, fretting uselessly. Russel tried again and again. Nathaniel was getting agitated, and I started to freak out. Pacing, mumbling, praying—I was a basket case.

Gurgling noises were coming from Nathaniel, a sound Russel described later as a death gurgle. At the time he tried to reassure us both by saying, "The bubbling means he's breathing."

When he realized he wasn't going to succeed, Russel instructed me to call 911. Shaking in panic, I dialed the number. They said, "What is the address of the emergency?"

"Nine one one!" I screamed repeatedly, telling the operator the number I had just dialed instead of the address where we wanted the ambulance to come, which was not exactly helpful. Russel grabbed the phone and gave her the address.

Later I would look back at this as the moment when I knew what role Russel would play in our family. I could handle the day-to-day, but in an emergency, I fell apart. Russel had been a lifeguard and a camp counselor—he knew CPR even though he'd never actually had to use it. Usually he was very emotional—he'd often cry after a rough medical moment—but in an emergency, Russel was the one you wanted by your side. He remembered everything the doctors told us. Even when he didn't know what to do, or couldn't get it right the first time, he stayed calm and confident. He took charge. No matter how bad the situation got, no matter how tense and gross, Russel knew exactly how to manage and how to keep Nathaniel safe until we got to a medical professional.

Finally, the ambulance came and took us to a local hospital, where they replaced the trach. He didn't need surgery, but it was a painful procedure.

As Nathaniel got older, we started teaching him how to keep himself safe. Whenever he started to fiddle with his trach or his g-tube—we called them his buttons—I'd say, "No, don't touch. It's not a toy, be careful." It was like what most parents do with a baby and a hot stove, except imagine that there are three burners on and the stove is within the baby's reach at all times.

Mileboulders

NATHANIEL Having Treacher Collins meant that my tongue continued to grow normally, but my jaw didn't. In order for me to start eating through my mouth and to continue breathing through it, the doctors had to expand my jaw. I bet you're wondering, *How do they expand someone's jaw?* The answer, unfortunately, is that they have to imitate the way your body grows naturally, so they do it little by little, over many years. Which translates to: slowly, painfully, through many surgeries.

MAGDA Alongside the normal developmental milestones that parents have for their kids—sitting, babbling, crawling, doing puzzles, and so on, we had bigger ones we were trying to reach. *Mileboulders*. A big one was to feed Nathaniel through his mouth.

Not long after we moved to Long Island, when Nathaniel was six months old, he had his first mandibular distraction, the surgery to expand his jaw. Dr. McCarthy had, with colleagues, pioneered this surgery to help kids like Nathaniel. Dr. McCarthy was kind of a god in our new world.

Nathaniel came home from the surgery with pins in his jaw that had to be turned every day in order to gently stretch the bone and allow new bone to fill the space. "Pins." "Gently." "Stretch." These are the words the doctors used, and they made the procedure sound rather relaxing, like yoga, or crafting, but this miracle of modern medicine looked and felt more like medieval torture.

NATHANIEL It's too bad that my dad was traveling a lot at the time and after the surgery my mom was the one who had to turn the pins. My dad is much better at that stuff. My mom doing gross medical procedures is a bit like a fish riding a bicycle. But worse. She tells me that when it was time to tighten the screws in my jaw, she would begin by crying and throwing up.

Good start. Then she would put me on the floor and kneel on top of me, with her knees on my hands to keep me from moving. Nice. Basically, no matter how loving and gentle she was, if someone had looked through the window they would have called Child Protective Services when they saw her following the doctor's orders.

When she turned the tiny screwdriver, blood would trickle down the side of my head. Same thing on the other side. There are no photos of this in our albums, which is too bad. It was probably such a sorry sight that I could win a "least cute baby photo" contest. When my mom finished, she'd throw up one more time for good measure, then we'd go on our merry way until the next day, when she had to do it all over again.

When you think about it, it's pretty crazy to be tortured by your own loving mother when you're an infant. The same person who cuddles you 99 percent of the time, then takes a screwdriver, sits on top of you, and hurts you. My mom says I cried in pain every time. I don't remember any of it, but I guess that because my parents did it with love, not out of anger or rage, I wasn't psychologically damaged. My grandmother says that babies feel energy. So maybe these experiences scarred me. But maybe they made me strong. Maybe both. All I can report is that I'm okay so far.

MÁGDA   Just because his jaw was slightly bigger after the surgery didn't mean that Nathaniel automatically understood how to eat. I'd put baby food on a spoon and he'd hold it in his mouth—delicious!—but he didn't get that the idea was to swallow it. He'd never had to wrap his young head around the concept of swallowing. If I pushed food down his throat, he'd choke.

A therapist came over twice a week to help Nathaniel learn how to swallow. Nathaniel was really into it, mostly because the therapy involved a strange spoon-like utensil which she used to feed him peanut butter, Cool Whip and Nutella, all of which are still among his favorite "foods," if you can call them that. The little tastes that she managed to feed him weren't enough to live on, so we were still using the g-tube to give him formula, which he was still throwing up violently. At four months old, Nathaniel had a surgery called a *fundoplication*, which makes it harder for food to come up the wrong way. It helped for a while, but over time it had loosened. Now the doctors scheduled a second surgery to tighten it. Russel wanted to know when they were going to put the "fun" in "fundoplication."

NATHANIEL   I love to eat, so I feel sorry for my baby self when I think of all that yummy food I missed. My mom tells me stories about how differently she ate as a child because she likes me to know about her childhood, but it also reminds me that even though I spent some time eating through a tube, people eat differently all over the world.

ZAP! FLASHBACK!

MAGDA   My father grew vegetables and fruit on the farm, but for some reason the Russian government, which had occupied Poland since World War II, did not want us to have control over the groceries in our lives, starting with meat. If you wanted to keep your own pig, you had to hide it illegally. My mother kept a few chickens in hiding so we could have eggs. Most everything else at the supermarket was rationed, meaning each family only got a limited amount every week, such as two pounds of red meat, two pounds of kielbasa, two pounds of pork, and one pound of chicken. This meat did not sit in the butcher's refrigerator, available for purchase. Instead, the store would receive a limited amount twice a week. If you got to the store at five in the morning to wait on line, you might get a better quality of kielbasa, or there would still be some chicken left. But if you didn't get there until eight, you might have to wait on line for three hours only to score a very fatty piece of meat, barely good enough for broth, or go home empty-handed. The same was true for sugar. And toilet paper.

Sometimes, if a neighbor slaughtered a contraband pig, my father would secretly trade vegetables and potatoes for a chunk of it. They'd bring it over to our house in the dark of night, after curfew, wearing dark clothes, and cut it up in the basement by flashlight. Ordinary people were driven to extremes to put a little meat on the table. Mostly we ate the vegetables and fruit that we grew on the farm. We went fishing and ate what we caught. And the greatest fun of all was mushroom picking.

NATHANIEL　As far back as I can remember, my mother has talked me through the hardest moments, distracting me when I was too uncomfortable after surgeries to do anything but listen, drifting in and out of sleep. My favorite stories, always, were the ones about her childhood in Poland. It sounded like another world, but pieces of it have been carried into my life: The soups. The squirrel in the cabbage. The mushrooms.

ZAP! FLASHBACK!

MAGDA　The mushroom season only lasts for a couple months at the end of the summer. My father would wake us up at three in the morning. (My mother never came with us. Someone had to stay home to sell tomatoes and make sure people didn't jump the fence and steal food from the farm. Once my mother stopped a thief who tried to steal all our shoes. She beat him with a broom and called the police.)

With little backpacks that my mother packed full of lunch and snacks, carrying cute, woven baskets, we drove to the woods. By the time we got there, it was dawn. We watched the sun come up and headed straight into the wilderness. There were no trails, but my father had a great sense of direction. No matter how far we wandered, he could always find his way out. He knew where and how to find mushrooms, even when we hadn't been there for a while. He showed us which mushrooms were poisonous and which were the best ones, the ones considered to be the top of the mushroom royal family. Cheap ones grew on top of tree stumps. The higher quality ones knew better—they hid in the moss. Mushrooms that were spongy under the cap were tastier than those with slits under the cap. The very best was the *prawdziwek*, which means "the real mushroom." The three of us—the oldest of the six kids who would eventually form our family—would race through the woods, competing for who brought in the best haul.

It was always an adventure. On one rainy day I lost a shoe in the mud. The first time my youngest brother, Michal, joined us, he stood up and said, "What's that? Something's hitting my boot!"

It was a snake, striking his boot again and again. He was so little he had no idea what that long, skinny wiggling thing was.

We'd get home around ten in the morning, clean the mushrooms, cut them up, and spread them out to air-dry on something I can only call a Help-Mushrooms-Air-Dry machine.

Some mushrooms went into jars of sauce. Others were reserved for soup. My mother kept some dried mushrooms in a special cotton sack for use throughout the year, and the rest were pickled. She made the best pickled mushrooms.

The work we put into collecting the mushrooms and harvesting the produce gave the food we ate deeper meaning. As we ate it, we felt the satisfaction of having found it.

I love to cook with mushrooms, but the farmed ones at the grocery store don't compare to what I grew up eating, so my family ships me dried mushrooms in Ziploc bags, and every time someone comes to visit from Poland, they sneak some through customs, and I try to make my house smell as good as when my mother made them.

> No matter how hard-won our food was, meals were always loud, with me, my two siblings who were closest in age, and often cousins at the table, full of chatter, laughter, and the clinking of cutlery. This is what family was to me. I wanted Nathaniel to have that. I wanted him off the g-tube and up at the table.

MÁGDA When Nathaniel was seven months old, my mother said, "Babies at this age should start eating real foods like apples and bananas." I liked the sound of real, whole foods like the ones we grew on our farm. Formula supposedly contained all the nutrients Nathaniel needed, but not if he kept throwing it all up. So I went rogue and tried sending some *real* food up through the g-tube.

First, I blended a little banana with water and put it into the tube. Miraculously, he kept it down! The next day, in the grocery store, I noticed other mothers pondering the long shelves full of jars of organic baby food. It looked so much more appealing than chemical formula, so I picked one up. Why shouldn't I try it? His stomach was like everyone else's (except for the damage caused by throwing up so much). I put a few jars in my cart, and that night I fed him some sweet potato mush through the g-tube. Again, he kept it down. I couldn't have been happier to know that I was finally nourishing my baby with food that I recognized as having come from the ground.

There's always a soup to be made. I quickly realized that I could water down whatever I made for dinner, blend it, and put it in the g-tube. For the first time in his life, Nathaniel had real food in his belly. He smelled the food as I loaded it in. The warm soups settled in his stomach, and I pretended to myself that he could somewhat taste the food. At the very least, he had to be burping up good flavors for the first time in his life.

Soon I was putting Nathaniel into his high chair to play with mashed-up bananas and mashed potatoes, get himself dirty, and be part of the family during dinner, even though he still wasn't really eating much. I counted calories, making sure he was getting enough protein, fruit, and vegetables. It was a lot of work, but I refused to believe he'd go through life with a tube in his stomach.

At last, he started gaining weight. He was still very thin, but he was thriving.

The day came when he was scheduled to have the second fundoplication.

Nathaniel was eight months old and had been eating real food for about six weeks. The hospital staff prepped him, took his vitals, and set up the IV. He was in his little green gown and socks, and Russel was in his scrubs ready to carry Nathaniel into the OR as he always did. As we walked toward the operating room, the doctor turned to me and asked, "What's new?"

Dr. Ginsburg, who had been the one to put Nathaniel's g-tube in, was a tall, proud, handsome guy who had a reputation for odd bedside manners. The nurses told us he never opened up to patients, but we found him to be very friendly. When our paths crossed in the hospital hallways, he always stopped to ask how we were doing.

Now I told the doctor that Nathaniel had started eating real food and was keeping it down.

"That's good news! When did he last throw up?" the doctor asked.

"About a month ago," I told him.

We were in the middle of the hospital hallway. Dr. Ginsburg stopped in his tracks. There was nearly a comical pileup as the rest of us halted behind him. He said, "He's keeping everything down! What are you doing here? Go home!" He instructed the nurses to remove the IV and told me to dress Nathaniel and take him home. "I'm not going to mess with him," he said.

| NATHANIEL | That guy sounds like my kind of doctor. The kind who'd rather not mess with me.

To Hear

NATHANIEL I've had a hearing aid for as long as I can remember. My mom's love for music made my hearing really important to her, but, in spite of her efforts, I never really took to it. I didn't have any interest in piano lessons. In fact, our piano is in the garage right now because we don't have room for it in the house, but that's still kind of strange when you know that my mom was a very serious pianist for a long time. Mom says the reason she gave up playing is because when we were little, every time she sat down to play, one of us wanted to sit on her lap and bang on the keys. When I did it, I had Thomas trains in each fist. She was afraid I would break the keys. Sorry about that, Mom.

MÁGDA The first thing I had noticed when Nathaniel was born was that he was missing ears. Growing up as a pianist, I was told that I had "a good ear," but it didn't mean my ears looked special in any way. A good ear meant I heard detail and layers and pitch and timbre and understood how they lent themselves to music. Was I born with a good ear? It's hard to say. I started playing piano when I was so young that nobody knows if I was born with my ear for music or if it was learned.

NATHANIEL It's amazing to hear about a time when my mother's life revolved around music, now that it revolves around her family. It makes me think about how much my life will change over the years.

ZAP! FLASHBACK!

MÁGDA Right next to my parents' farm was a house that has since been torn down. It was an old-fashioned little wooden house, painted black. My great-aunt Helena—my father's aunt—lived there alone, with a grand piano and a small, fluffy white dog named Booba. Her house seemed extravagant to me, full of velvets, with beautiful, draped curtains. Every sofa was covered in huge, elaborately dressed dolls that we weren't allowed to touch. My aunt sewed fancy dresses for everyone in town, and she herself dressed like a movie star, in dresses of her creation, stylish hats, and fancy shoes.

When I was around three or four years old, my twin cousins, who were about my age, lived in the second-floor apartment of our house while their father, my uncle, built a house in the forest. They stayed upstairs in my grandmother's apartment but we all shared a kitchen. My great-aunt, who had gone to a conservatory (a music school) in Ukraine, started teaching the three of us piano. She would show us something to play, then we would take turns trying it out.

I entered my first piano competition when I was almost five. We took a train to a nearby town—my first train ride—and when I signed in, I could barely write my first name. But I won some prize in my age group, and from then on, my life was filled with going from one competition to another.

This was a mentality people in my community had at the time—maybe it was a Russian thing—every child was expected to specialize in something. One of my sisters played cello. She was very talented, but a bit lazy. One of my brothers was a genius in biology, winning science competitions all over the country. Once piano was determined to be my talent, I spent the rest of my childhood focused on it. I went to school in the morning, then home for lunch, then to music school all afternoon. There was no school bus to either school, and my mother was too busy to drive me, so I walked almost four miles a day, rain, snow, or shine. Sometimes I would catch the town bus, but waiting for it might take twenty minutes. It was never worth it. So in addition to my full school schedule, I spent about two hours a day commuting by foot. If I had a math test, I had to wake up at three in the morning to study for it.

When a competition was coming up, the music school would write a letter excusing me from regular school. Then they'd occassionally lock us in a practice room for eight hours a day. Some kids would jump out of the second-floor window onto the grassy yard and sneak into town. I'd look out the window and see my friends waving, "Come on, Magda, let's go." It was tempting, but I never joined them. I was afraid of heights.

NATHANIEL When I was born, everyone focused on helping me breathe and eat first. Eventually, when I was bigger and more stable, they turned their attention to my hearing. The better I could hear, the sooner I'd learn to talk.

MAGDA When Nathaniel was only a few months old, Dr. Bernstein pushed us to get him a hearing aid. Though Nathaniel had no ears to channel noise, just a tiny flap of skin, the good news was that his inner ear was perfectly fine. He was a great candidate for a device called a Bone-Anchored Hearing Aid (BAHA). The BAHA is a hearing aid that carries sound vibrations directly through your bone to your inner ear. If you think it sounds impossible that sound vibrations could run through your bones and convert to words in your brain, I agree. But I feel the same way about the miracle of TV screens.

There were good reasons to wait until he was older to give Nathaniel this hearing aid. A big one was cost. Insurance only covered the first $500 of a hearing aid, but the BAHA cost $5,000, and if it broke, we had to replace it. I'm not a math whiz, but anyone could see that wasn't a great deal. However, the doctors told us that the longer a child goes without being able to hear well, the more difficulty he has learning to speak. The earlier we gave Nathaniel sound, the better shot he had at talking easily and clearly. We didn't know if I'd been born with a good ear or had developed it through my piano training. Now, I wanted Nathaniel's hearing to get an early opportunity of a different sort.

So we followed Dr. Bernstein's suggestion and scheduled Nathaniel to get his BAHA at NYU. Beforehand, the hearing specialist told us, "Some babies cry when we put it on because they're not used to such loud noises around them. We'll try it for two minutes, and if he gets upset we'll take it off."

The doctor handed me the hearing aid and showed me how to turn it on. For now, while he was a baby and then a toddler, it would be held on his head by a tight headband. When I slid the band around his head, Nathaniel started fussing, as if to say, "What are you doing to me?" The headband had to be really tight.

Then I turned the hearing aid on. We didn't know what to expect, but as soon as we spoke quietly to him,

Nathaniel's face lit up instantly. His eyes got wide. He smiled and looked around with happy curiosity.

He started babbling, then looked startled at the sound of his own voice. It must have been much louder than what he was used to. His face brightened, and he babbled more. Everything about his face said, "This is a miracle." Russel started crying, he was so happy.

After a bit, because the doctor didn't want to over-stimulate him, I took the hearing aid off. The corners of Nathaniel's mouth immediately turned down. He reached toward me. He wanted it back!

Seeing the joy on his face made me realize how much we take our own hearing for granted. I suddenly felt grateful. For all those years I had played the piano, I had never appreciated my hearing as a gift, like every sense, one of the miracles of life that most of us experience every day.

From that moment on, Nathaniel did not want to take his BAHA off. Ever. If we tried, he'd start crying. He eventually got used to the idea that it had to come off for sleep and baths, but as soon as he woke up or finished a bath, he'd look around for it and make it clear that he wanted it. I had to add a backup battery to the list of supplies I carried at all times. When the battery died, he'd cry and point to his hearing aid.

Later, when Nathaniel was around two-and-a-half and potty training, his hearing aid accidentally fell into the toilet. That's right, the $5,000 hearing aid, which was so sensitive to moisture that he couldn't even wear it out in the rain. The stretchy headband that held it on tended to loosen over time and occasionally needed to be replaced. Lucky us, it must have been stretched out enough to fall off at the worst possible moment. Nathaniel was horrified. Even though he was little, he knew what a disaster this was. He immediately started wailing, "I want my hearing aid!"

Thankfully, I was there with him in the bathroom. In one of my least favorite but still heroic moments, I reached into the toilet full of pee and grabbed the hearing aid. I quickly swiped it with a disinfectant wipe and dropped it into the dehumidifying container where it ordinarily lived at night. Three hours later, it was miraculously restored.

I'd been playing piano for Nathaniel since he was born, but now that he could hear clearly, I made my selections more deliberately. I chose music and composers the same way you pick different books to stretch different parts of your mind: Bach, which is very mathematically constructed. Debussy, which is more like impressionist painting.

I picked a few pieces to play over and over again so he would learn to recognize them. Nathaniel loved Debussy's "Arabesque." Even before he had his hearing aid, before I could tell if he was hearing it or feeling the vibrations, I had felt like playing music with him connected us. But it made all the difference to know for sure that he could hear, to see his face respond to what I was playing. Russel talks about how it lifted all of our spirits.

With the BAHA (we called it his "magic ear"), a new world of noise opened up. For the first time, he could hear dogs barking. Birds. Kids playing. Cars driving by. He reacted to everything. Before, when he watched TV shows, he had sat silently, but now, when he watched Baby Mozart videos or heard me play the piano, he danced and sang. And when he was still being fed for hours through the g-tube, I could put on a video and know that he wasn't bored out of his mind. He was a much happier child.

When you're taking care of a baby twenty-four hours a day, every new thing they do is extraordinary. That's why, as you may have noticed, every mom thinks her own child is a genius—because she saw the baby go from doing nothing but eating and sleeping to smiling, clapping, and learning to speak a whole language pretty fluently in just a few years. My baby's milestones weren't set in a straight road. They were a bit scattered and required some U-turns and detours. When Nathaniel got his hearing aid, he took a big leap forward. His personality came alive. His expression and joy made everything worth it.

| NATHANIEL | Sound travels through bone to your brain. Yeah, it was a surprise to me too. I've never spent much time thinking about how the hearing aid works, but I do get annoyed when I can't hear because, well, I can't hear. On the other hand, occasionally it's a plus to be able to tune everybody out. Sometimes, when I don't want to listen to my brother, I subtly turn the hearing aid off. It looks like I'm scratching my head, and Jacob has no clue. And another feature of the hearing aid is that I can hear any and everything around me, like if someone not too far away is whispering a secret. That's right. I would make an excellent spy.

A Little Brother

NATHANIEL My mom was the eldest of six siblings, and taking care of them helped her learn to be a mom. There are three older siblings, then a gap, then three younger siblings. My uncle Michal is the eldest of the youngest, if you know what I mean. He's the fourth child, and he's fifteen years younger than my mom! Even though she was a busy high school student and musician, she loved having a baby brother. Every day she hurried home between school and music school to spend time with him. Basically, Michal was her practice baby.

MAGDA While I was at school, my mother brought baby Michal with her everywhere, to weed the garden, to pick tomatoes. She'd lug a hand-me-down ExerSaucer around and let him bounce while he watched her work. When I took over, I immediately pushed his stroller straight into the woods. This was our routine for the first few years of his life, while I was in high school. We'd off-road it, bumping the stroller over tree roots and through gullies. I'd point to knotholes in the trees and tell him, "This is where the elves live. They go down through the tree to their underground world." Then I'd kneel next to him and say, "Oh my God! I just saw a little elf! Did you see it scamper back into the tree? They're so fast!"

Michal would say, "Oh yes, I saw his little hat."

I was already away at college when my two younger sisters were born, but Michal was only eleven years older than Nathaniel, so Nathaniel is right, in a way he felt like my second baby.

I always wanted to have a big family. After the surprise of Nathaniel, we had to think carefully about having a second child. First, we needed to feel settled. After the gloomy basement where we spent Nathaniel's first year, we moved to Charlotte, North Carolina. Our new backyard in Charlotte had a patio and a sunny patch where Nathaniel and I planted a flower garden. Beyond the garden was a steep hill, at the top of which was a muddy play area. Every morning I slowly sipped coffee while Nathaniel played in the dirt with his Tonka trucks. We were both happy to be out of the basement, spending the sunny warm mornings in the fresh air.

When Russel was at work, Nathaniel and I walked around the neighborhood to the playground or the kiddie pool. This was Nathaniel's first pool experience and though I had to be very careful that his trach didn't get wet, he absolutely loved swimming.

When Nathaniel was nearly two years old we were supposed to fly to New York for his second jaw surgery. There was a huge snowstorm on the East Coast, and all the flights were canceled, but the surgery wasn't. We had to be at the hospital at six in the morning, so we decided to drive. It was a twelve-hour drive with stops to feed him and change his diaper.

By the time we got to Virginia, the roads were very slippery. We stopped at a mall that had a Sears to try to buy snow tires. They told us it would be a two-hour wait, so we entertained Nathaniel by walking around the mall. We found a book store with a train table, and he played there happily while the tires were changed, so before we got back on the road I bought a Thomas the Tank Engine DVD to keep him occupied for the remainder of the trip. The DVD was *Percy Takes the*

Plunge, and it came with a green Percy train. Nathaniel was immediately obsessed with that video. He watched it again and again for the rest of the drive. In New York, in order to entertain him after the surgery, I bought him more Thomas DVDs and books.

At home, after that second jaw surgery, Nathaniel had to sit still for hours while nutrients slowly made their way through the g-tube into his body. His new train table helped him through it. After that, he got a new train or two after every surgery, and he would spend countless hours slowly being fed and playing with the trains. We didn't have anything fancy in our lives, but our son had a very impressive collection of trains.

Once I finally (finally!) passed the driving test to get my license, some days I would drop Russel off at work and take Nathaniel to story time at the bookstore. This store also had a Thomas the Tank Engine table where he was content to play for hours. He wasn't the only Thomas-obsessed kid, so he made a couple of "train" friends, and the mothers and I would smile at each other, sometimes exchanging sympathetic words about our children's shared obsession with speaking trains who don't have very dramatic lives. In North Carolina, Nathaniel and I found company. Friends.

Life was pretty good, and we started thinking it might be nice for Nathaniel to have a little brother or sister. I always wanted to have at least two kids so they could play with each other like my siblings and cousins and I did.

Russel and I were worried that we would have another kid with Treacher Collins. That might seem like a pretty harsh thing to say, or even rude to Nathaniel, but we weren't saying we didn't want *Nathaniel*! It's just that caring for Nathaniel required lots of time and money and plain old energy. Having another child with special needs felt like it would be too much for all of us. And—this is the most important part—Nathaniel agrees. The last thing he would have wanted was a sibling who took us away from him.

When I tell you how difficult it was in the beginning, I want to be clear about something: The biggest reason I was so upset by Nathaniel's birth was because I had no idea what was coming. How he looked and the hurdles he faced were something I could accept and love, but the shock was gigantic. When life takes a sudden unexpected turn, we are asked to show what we are made of. It took me time to find my balance. That can be true in so many ways in life. In planning for Jacob, we couldn't afford any more surprises.

When I was twenty weeks pregnant, the doctor took a 4D image to measure his head, jaw, and ears. You could clearly see his features. An ear! The most noticeable trait in Treacher Collins is the malformed ear, so when I saw that ear I knew deep in my heart that Jacob was okay, whatever "okay" means.

Now that I'm pretty much an expert on Treacher Collins, now that both my boys are strong and independent, now that there are so many more resources and new technologies available to families of a child with Treacher Collins, I feel differently. I would care for a baby with severe issues all over again. I'd be proud and honored to do it. Ten-years-ago me would be astounded.

The fact that our second son would be genetically "normal" in our family meant that he was going to need less, and that he was going to get less. That would be his blessing and burden. In our family, Jacob wasn't "different." He was the "normal" one. But it's never that simple. For Jacob, having a special brother would shape his life. It would make *his* life different too.

NATHANIEL   What is normal? If one person can fly, but no one else can do it, then it's not normal. So, does that mean that everyone who can't fly is normal—even me? Of course not. There are many other ways to be different. In fact, there are so many other ways to be different that *everyone* is different. But for some reason lots of people decide that if you look like them and behave like them and have the same interests as them, then you meet their idea of "normal." When people don't see me as normal, they're focusing on a tiny piece of me—the outside, from the neck up—instead of seeing a fuller, cooler picture. There's nothing wrong with being unusual. Flying isn't normal, but it's better than walking. Having four dogs isn't normal, but it's better than three. Then again, I'm biased because I have four dogs.

MÁGDA Jacob came into the world in July of 2006 with ten fingers, ten toes, two ears, and with his own quirks and delights and needs. Doctors and nurses stopped by and congratulated me, saying, "Look at him, he looks like a doll." I didn't want to compare my children, but I couldn't help noticing how differently people behaved toward me and my newest little one.

So *this* was what most people experienced after having a baby—joy, pride, celebration. The horror movie audience was gone, and in their place was the cooing smiles of a heartwarming family flick. I wished that Nathaniel and I had gotten that kind of reception when he was born, and wondered if there was a way to have that experience even when your child had serious, unexpected complications.

The next day I was home, Jacob was nursing, Nathaniel was playing with his trains, and I said to Russel, "We are complete."

A Day Out with Thomas

NATHANIEL   I was two and a half when Jacob was born, and my parents tell me that I was excited to meet my brother, but it only took me two days, max, to get jealous. My mom was holding Jacob a lot, and I wasn't ready to share.

I said, "It's time for that baby to go back to the hospital," and I'm told that every now and then I would try to hit Jacob in the head with one of my trains. Or, the way I see it, Jacob's head probably got in the way of my train.

MAGDA   To help Nathaniel deal with the little blob who was now taking up so much of my time, I tried to stick with our familiar routines. We still went to the park every morning, first thing before it got too hot. Jacob would nap in the stroller while I pushed Nathaniel on the swings.

At dinnertime, the four of us sat around the table; Nathaniel had graduated to a regular chair, and Jacob used the high chair where Nathaniel had played with more food than he was able to eat. It was what families do all the time without even thinking: eating dinner together, squabbling, being told to take one more bite of broccoli, clamoring for dessert. It was what I'd grown up with in Poland without ever stopping to appreciate it, what I always expected to be my family life.

At night, we'd turn on the TV above the fireplace, switch the channel to *Baby Looney Tunes*, and all dance together, with me bouncing Jacob in my arms.

With a newborn baby, Nathaniel's medical issues, and my own health issues (more on that later), we barely left the house for the first year of Jacob's life. But gradually I started planning outings for me and the boys. We weren't exactly foraging for mushrooms the way I did as a child, but we spent lots of time at the local discovery museum in North Carolina. There was a big pile of dirt where they could dig and water tables where they could pan for gold. When the boys lost themselves in exploration, or when I collected books and stickers on a topic like butterflies or spiders—those were the moments when I felt like the boys were having a happy childhood like mine. I refused to treat Nathaniel as sickly or fragile. I didn't want that to be part of his identity.

Then I found a dream trip for the boys. There was a Thomas the Tank Engine–themed week at an amusement park two hours away. We would ride a life-size Thomas through the Blue Ridge Mountains, there would be storytelling, and afterward, if we were up to it, we could try out classic rides like a carousel and a Ferris wheel.

The Day Out with Thomas was a long-awaited treat for us—Nathaniel, three years old, had recovered from his most recent surgery and one-year-old Jacob was just getting big enough to enjoy such outings. We were all very excited.

The first thing that went wrong was that Jacob decided to hurl his pacifier out the window of the train. Then he immediately regretted that move. Being a toddler is hard that way. Jacob expressed his regret by howling for the entire rest of the ride. Then the train encountered a tree that had fallen across the tracks. We had to stop and return to the station going backwards. At the time, I assumed this was another hitch in our plans, although, looking back, it seems very possible that it was part of the ride, meant to add drama to our train ride. We were making plenty of drama all on our own.

It was our lucky day (I thought)—the gift shop at the end of the line had train-themed everything . . . and somehow among all that Russel found lollipops shaped like pacifiers. Soon Jacob was happily sucking and hopped up on sugar.

Toddler soothed at last, we were exploring the Thomas-themed park when I noticed that Nathaniel's shirt was wet around his belly. At first I thought he was sweating, but soon Russel and I realized that every sip of water he took was spilling right out of his stomach! His g-tube had been dislodged. It was yucky and dangerous.

With a cloth diaper wrapped around Nathaniel's stomach and Jacob loudly protesting being in the car seat, we sped to the hospital, three hours away, where they repaired the g-tube.

NATHANIEL A lot was going wrong, but the way I remember it, I tried to ignore all of that and have some fun. There were trains all around me, and I was obsessed. The chaos of my baby brother screaming and crying and the small issue of my stomach leaking were distractions for the grownups to deal with. I played happily while they called doctors and comforted Jacob and did all the worrying and problem-solving.

MAGDA Not long after the Thomas the Train debacle, we removed the g-tube. It was a very quick surgery, but a huge day—one less hole in Nathaniel's body. Now he could go down the slide on his belly the way he wanted to, and he didn't have to worry about it catching on the edge of a table. He had been cautious about this foreign part of his body for all of his first four years—"Be careful! Watch your g-tube!"—when all he should have been thinking about was playing and avoiding skinned knees.

We celebrated at Cheesecake Factory, Nathaniel's favorite restaurant at the time. I felt like the sky was smiling. We were another step closer to "normal."

NATHANIEL   I don't remember getting my g-tube out, but I spent years being careful about my trach and my hearing aid, so I know how good it must have felt to have one less thing to worry about. And I am always up for cheesecake.

PART II
A HAPPY CHILDHOOD

Meet Nathaniel

NATHANIEL I started school in kindergarten, like most other kids. My parents say that even though I had lots of doctors' appointments, they wanted me to start school with everyone else. Personally, I think enrolling me in ninja warrior camp would have been a little more original.

My parents tried really hard to make sure the other kids understood what was going on with me and accepted me, so that's what my mom talks about when she describes my school experience. Funny thing is that the *more* time my parents spent preparing the parents and kids, the *less* time I had to spend thinking about and explaining how I was different. Because they made a big deal of it, it wasn't a big deal to me at all. If that makes sense.

We were a little nervous about Nathaniel starting school. At the playground, in movie theaters, on the street, kids had started to point at him saying, "Eeewww." Some of them would cry and ask to leave. Parents were sometimes embarrassed by this, but we didn't judge it. It's natural to have a reaction when someone looks dramatically different.

We moved to Connecticut around the time Nathaniel was ready to go to kindergarten. We knew that his facial difference would be a surprise to his classmates. The summer before school began, we contacted the principal, Dr. DePalma. We told her that we had a child with some issues and that we'd like to bring him in for a meeting.

Dr. DePalma, a petite Italian-American woman, happened to be the best principal that walked this planet. She made it clear that she was thrilled to have Nathaniel at the school.

Russel told her that he had an idea that he wanted to run past her. He said, "What if we write a letter to the school community? It could explain why Nathaniel looks the way he does. Maybe it would help everyone start off on the right foot."

Dr. DePalma loved the idea, and later, when she read his draft, she said, "This is brilliant. I can't wait." Her praise made Russel and me feel glad and proud that we'd found a good way to introduce our son to the community.

Russel wrote the letter, but it was from Nathaniel's perspective:

```
Hi! My name is Nathaniel Newman. I am
in your son/daughter's class. I had a
really great idea. You see, I figure by
now your kid has maybe asked a few ques-
tions about me or talked about me when
he/she came home from school today. Bet
it would help if I told you a little
more about myself.
```

The letter explained Treacher Collins syndrome in such a way that if a parent read it to a young child, they would both have all their questions answered.

```
Treacher Collins makes it so that, when
you're growing in Mommy's belly, the
```

bones in your face forget to grow like the rest of your bones. What happened to me was a lot of my bones forgot to grow. AND I EVEN GREW SOME YOU'RE NOT SUPPOSED TO HAVE! All this, they tell me, sort of makes me a miracle! Cool, but a bit silly, because isn't every kid in our class a miracle? Here is some of the different stuff about me:

- I have no ears. But, here is the amazing part, I hear everything you do! The stuff inside my head that makes you hear (drum, bones, nerves) are all there. Just no flippy-floppy ears on the outside. This is called "microtia." How do I hear, you ask? I have an amazing thing called a BAHA hearing aid. I call it my magic ear. It's a small brown thing that I wear on a colorful headband.

- I have no cheekbones and my eyes slant down because there aren't enough bones holding up my eyeballs! They say they can fix this when I'm older. I'm not in a rush because that means another trip to NYU Medical Center. I've had like twenty surgeries there. I think that's plenty for now!

- My jawbone is really, really small. So is the inside of my mouth. The shape of my mouth, palate, throat, and airway is all a bit different. As a baby it was hard for me to eat and breathe, but I figured it out and now I eat like all the other kids at school.

One really serious thing I have to tell you about: Remember I said I have some extra bones? Mine grew in a pretty yucky place. The back of my nose! I got a really cute nose on the outside, but on the inside there's a wall of solid bone at the back. This one has a hard name to say: Complete Bilateral Choanal Atresia. It does make some stuff real hard for me. Especially breathing. That is why they put a hole in my throat with a cool tube sticking out of it. It's called a tracheostomy. At school, I wear a nifty purple cap over it so I can still talk real loud and it helps me keep dirt out.

NATHANIEL Unfortunately, that "nifty purple cap" looked like a toy. Kids were always trying to pull it out. "I want to wear your necklace," they'd say, then grab at it and pull. My weapon of choice to defend myself was one I had tested on my brother with good results: a Thomas & Friends toy train. For a couple of years, I always had Percy in one hand.

MAGDA The letter was already too long, but better too much than too little. We gave the parents suggestions for instructions they might give their kids: not to stare and not to touch the trach or hearing aid. We also explained that because of his nose being blocked, sometimes Nathaniel's nose ran and he didn't notice it. If his nose was running, instead of laughing at him, the kids could just tell him to wipe it and he would.

Finally, we asked them to treat Nathaniel like everyone else. We told them Treacher Collins didn't impact his mental or emotional development. And we said they could call us with questions.

The letter helped set up Nathaniel for an easy entry into kindergarten. Everyone knew that a kid who was different was in the class, nobody would be taken off guard, the parents would have a chance to prepare their kids and answer questions, and we could avoid some of the extra stares.

If you think about it, how many kids head off to school hoping their classmates will embrace their differences and welcome them? Maybe it doesn't start as young as kindergarten, but most kids have doubts and insecurities on the inside, whereas Nathaniel's struggles were out on display. Wouldn't it be great if everyone could write a letter to their future classmates saying, "Here are the unusual things about me. Please don't be scared. Ask me anything you want. I just want to make friends and play."

Even though his kindergarten classmates were perfectly nice to him, from the very beginning Nathaniel's school experience was different from other kids'. A nurse had to be within a few feet of him at all times. The g-tube was gone, but he had that very expensive hearing aid that couldn't get wet or damaged, and the tracheostomy, which had to be suctioned if it got clogged, or immediately replaced if it got dislodged. If a kid tried to grab the tempting trach button, the nurse was there to intervene.

NATHANIEL The nurse was Keeper of the Suction. She shadowed me constantly. Every so often one would go off to another job and a new one would show up. Some of the nurses tried to make conversation, but mostly they hovered nearby. I didn't pay much attention to them. When you're six years old, teachers and your parents are already watching over you most of the time. What's one more person? The nurse would suction me when I needed it, and I'd return to whatever I was doing.

My mom tells me that on the first day of kindergarten, she came to the classroom to introduce me to the other kids. We all sat in a circle on the rug, and I can imagine it pretty clearly because I've seen her say this to kids a million times now.

She starts by asking, "Do you want to know why Nathaniel looks like this? It's just the way he was born." Then she tells them: "Touch your face. Feel your cheekbones. Nathaniel doesn't have cheekbones like you. That's why he looks different. That button on his neck helps him breathe. Please don't touch it. And the other button, over here, is his hearing aid."

When she finished explaining me to my kindergarten class, she asked if there were any questions.

"I'm scared of him," one boy said. (It's not what I would call a question, but whatever.)

"I'm sorry you feel that way," my mom said. "Why are you scared?"

"He looks scary," the boy said. Kindergarteners have a way with words.

Mom said, "He looks different, but different doesn't have to be scary."

As Mom tells it, I wasn't very involved in the conversation. I just said hi and smiled at the other kids, but wasn't dying to talk to them about how different I was. That sounds about right.

Good Neighbors

MÁGDA Dr. DePalma was wonderful and the school community was supportive, but outside of that warm, accepting space, the beginning of elementary school was the worst point in Nathaniel's life when it came to being out in public.

Children are naturally curious. Most of us all learn to control our reactions as we get older and are more sensitive to the feelings of the people around us. "Learn" is the key word here. If a kid looked at Nathaniel with fear, curiosity, or a mix, I spoke to them the same way I spoke to the children in his class: "This is Nathaniel. He's six years old. He was born this way. Do you want to know what's going on with his face? He has a syndrome called Treacher Collins . . ."

The goal was to help parents and children to move past that moment of discomfort as quickly as possible so they could see Nathaniel for who he was. Just like we did.

NATHANIEL When kids stared at me, I didn't notice. If I noticed, I ignored it. Lots of times my dad or brother would mention it later, and only then would I realize that something they thought was notable had happened. My dad always said that it was the parents' job to teach their children to be kind, and most of the time a parent would say something like, "There's no reason to be scared of this boy. You can just ask him his name. What's your name?"

Then there were the clueless parents. They annoyed my dad. When he was in a good mood, he'd say to the parent, "This is a teachable moment. Instead of letting your kid say, 'Ooh, you look terrible. Were you in an accident? A fire?' you can tell your kid that it's okay to say, 'Do you mind if I ask you a question? What's that on your neck?'" That worked pretty well.

But sometimes my dad got frustrated with some-one—never a little kid—but an older kid or a grownup. He didn't feel like teaching people good behavior all day long. Then he would do what he calls a stare stop-per. All of a sudden, he would whip his head around and bark right in their face. I'm not sure how he came up with that one. Maybe he saw a dog do it to scare someone away and it worked. Dogs are pretty wise, so if that's where he was getting his ideas, I wasn't going to argue.

MAGDA Jacob remembers being very small, and seeing little kids stare wide-eyed at Nathaniel for up to two solid minutes. If they asked their parents what was on his brother's neck, sometimes Jacob would answer. But if they started reaching for the trach, he would put his small body between them, defending Nathaniel until the nearest grownup took charge. When he got older, he liked to do the stare stopper with Russel.

Sometimes it was hard for Russel to hold back.

A kid would say, "Oh my God, you're a freak! You're a monster!"

If a parent didn't step in to correct the kid, Russel would go up to him or her and say, "You heard what your child said and you're just sitting there."

The parent might respond, "What do you expect him to say? He's just a kid."

"Yes, he's just a kid, and you're his parent. It's your job to give him a different perspective." This happened two or three times every week, and it brought Russel to the edge. One time he came home and told me that he was about to sock some rude father, but he looked at Nathaniel and saw absolute fear in his eyes. Nathaniel didn't like seeing his father so angry.

Russel said, "All Nathaniel wanted to do was play and be happy and have fun and I was about to punch a middle-aged dad in the face because he was too stupid to teach his kid to be kind. I thought, *Whoa, this is exactly what I don't want him to do when people treat him badly*, and I stopped myself."

NATHANIEL Because I let insults roll over my shoulders, I don't remember too many stories about those incidents, but there's one that I do remember, probably because my parents kept telling people about it.

At the end of second grade, my dad changed jobs again, and we moved from Connecticut back to Charlotte. It was the end of October, almost Halloween, and Dad took me and Jacob to get frozen yogurt. It was one of those places where you can pick a bunch of toppings and trick out your yogurt. Mine was drowning in peanut butter cups, my favorite. We sat down outside to enjoy our desserts when a grownup came up to me and said, "Wow, where did you get such a cool mask? I wish I had a mask like that for

Halloween." Dumb, right? But this guy looked like he thought he'd just made the funniest joke in the world.

My dad was about to explode. I know because he told me afterward. But even though he sometimes loses it, he's taught me to be polite. So I smiled at the guy and said, "It's not a mask. It's my face." I just hit him with the simple facts. Then I went back to eating my yogurt. It was outstanding.

MAGDA Because Nathaniel didn't care, the rude comments never changed how our family operated. Our family went wherever we wanted to go and did whatever we wanted to do, and Nathaniel himself did the same without worrying about how strangers might react. We handled the rude reactions the way we would handle poison ivy. Unpleasant, unwelcome, but easily soothed.

There was only one other time Russel came very close to getting in a real fight over Nathaniel. When we returned to Charlotte, I thought I knew what to expect from our neighborhood—it was not far from where we'd lived the first time we were in Charlotte—but one woman ruined it. The only person who really hurt Nathaniel tremendously wasn't a bully—not someone at school or a kid in the neighborhood. It was our neighbor, a mother I'll call Liz.

Our house was in a gated community with six thousand houses, all with a similar layout but painted in different pastel colors. There were lots of kids in the neighborhood who played together after school and all summer long. Directly across the street from our house lived a boy named Luke who was Nathaniel's age. When the neighborhood kids played in a group, Nathaniel and this kid got along just fine. But soon it became clear that his mother, Liz, had problems with Nathaniel.

Her son had a trampoline in their backyard. We could see it from the upstairs balcony of our house, and one day Nathaniel spotted a bunch of neighborhood kids playing there. He went over and rang the doorbell.

When Liz answered the door she said, "We didn't make plans for a playdate today, Nathaniel. Luke is busy." I could hear her from our doorway. She used a friendly, authoritative mom voice. "We'll make plans another day," she said, and sent him away as if this were the way the world worked and he just didn't know it yet.

But there were no other kids left in the neighborhood for Nathaniel to play with. All of them were already playing together at that one house. Nathaniel came home crying.

At school, Luke told Nathaniel that he wanted to be friends, but his mother wouldn't let him. Maybe a mother wouldn't want her son to be friends with someone who was violent or rude or destructive, but Nathaniel was a sweet kid. He really never got in trouble except for trying to hit Jacob on the head when his brother was an infant. No other violence, I promise. The only reason for this woman to shun him was that she was uncomfortable with the way he looked!

As you already know, I had infinite understanding for any child having this reaction. A young person might need some time and guidance to get used to Nathaniel. But in this case the boy wasn't the issue. His *mother* was the one who couldn't handle it. What made me especially mad was that this was a woman who took pride in going to church every Sunday. Didn't she know that Christ's Golden Rule was "Do unto others as you would have them do unto you"?

When it was Luke's birthday, Liz went so far as to arrange two parties. One was at her house and included Nathaniel. Another took place outside the house—maybe they went bowling or to a playspace. Nathaniel wasn't invited to the second party, even though every other kid in the neighborhood went to both. This absolutely mystified us.

Russel, who is the opposite of shy, asked her directly, "Why did you invite my kid to one party and not the other?"

She said, "It's my son's special day. If Nathaniel were there it would take attention away from him."

When I heard that, I was speechless.

Russel and I tried to find a reasonable explanation for Liz's behavior: Maybe we're imagining this. Maybe Luke wasn't available when Nathaniel rang the doorbell, but then his schedule changed. Maybe there was only room for a limited number of guests at the second birthday party. Then Nathaniel befriended another neighborhood kid, Jake. Jake had Duchenne muscular dystrophy, a difficult, progressive disease. Russel found out from Jake's father that Liz treated Jake exactly the same way.

We tried to address it in a civilized fashion. We spoke to Liz and her husband in their home, explaining that our boys enjoyed playing with the neighborhood kids and that it would help for her to show her son how to be kind.

Liz said, "Being friends with Nathaniel is just too intense for Luke. I don't want him to have to deal with that." She actually made the argument that their difference was a good reason for limiting their time with her son!

One day Russel came home to find me and Nathaniel both upset over something Liz had done or said to him. It was the straw that broke the camel's back. Russel went upstairs to the balcony, waiting for Liz's husband to show up. When he did, Russel went down there, got up in his face, and yelled, "You'd better talk to your wife. My son is hysterically crying because of Liz and the way she treats him. He doesn't have enough to deal with? In my own house I have to worry about this?"

By this point the whole neighborhood could hear what was going on—I could see them peeking out of doorways and around hedges. Trouble in Pleasantville!

Russel went on, "She claims she's a good person, but she's evil. I'm not going to beat her up, but I'm going to beat you up if she doesn't stop treating my son like dirt."

I was embarrassed. "Please stop," I told Russel, and dragged him back to our house.

As we passed their next-door neighbor, he said, "Good for you, Russel, I hate that woman."

I ended up going over and apologizing to Liz and her husband for Russel's behavior. But knowing that any day she might do something else to hurt my son haunted me.

I did my best to prepare Nathaniel for how people might treat him. When I was growing up I read a book about the Polish piano prodigy Chopin. When he first performed publicly, at age eight, the audience who witnessed it went wild with appreciation of his genius. His mother, seeing that her little boy was overwhelmed by the attention, didn't want him to think of himself as such a standout. She said, "You are wearing a beautiful suit. They can't get over how handsome you are in this suit."

I remembered that story, and whenever Nathaniel asked, "Why are they staring at me?" I wouldn't say, "Because your face is out of whack." I'd say, "You're handsome. People are fascinated by your face. Everybody else looks like each other. Your eyes are different. You don't have cheekbones. You have almost no ears. They're curious. Where did this special boy come from?"

At night, when we were brushing teeth, I'd stand in front of the mirror with him. "Look at you, what do you think about your face?"

"Nothing."

I said, "Touch your eyes, they're beautiful and big. Look at your hair, it's lovely."

When there was an unpleasant incident, I'm sure some people would expect me to say, "Let's talk about what happened today. How did that make you feel?" That's one approach. But most of the time I didn't bring it up to Nathaniel. Instead of assuming he was upset or injured by other people's bad behavior and ignorance, I let him decide how he felt. I didn't expect him to be devastated. I didn't want him to dwell on it, and he didn't.

NATHANIEL   I don't spend time thinking about the way I look. The way I see it, Treacher Collins makes me unique. I wouldn't want it taken away from me, not even the hospital visits. (As far as I'm concerned missing school is highly underrated.) Treacher Collins is part, but not all, of who I am.

MAGDA   We went on. We got a dog. Nathaniel and Jake and the neighborhood kids spent hours together running around the neighborhood in superhero costumes that I had saved from Halloweens past. The kids played ball in their front yards or rode bikes on the street. In the afternoon, Nathaniel rode his miniature Jeep in a loop around the neighborhood. Every kid wanted a ride on that Jeep. One kid crashed into a wall, and after that Nathaniel wouldn't let anyone else drive, but he was happy to take them around. We had make-your-own pizza parties at our house. Nathaniel didn't think about Luke and his mother every day, but every time I walked out the door and saw her house, it reminded me of the possibility that any day of the week my son might be treated cruelly for no other reason than how he looked.

NATHANIEL I don't remember much from my childhood, but I remember Liz and Luke, especially one particular day on the school playground. Luke came up to me and told me that he liked me, but his mother wouldn't let him play with me. I can't remember what I said to Luke, but I'm pretty sure that in my head I was thinking, *That's stupid.*

My mom tells me that when I got home from school that day, I was upset. What Luke said was worse than a stare or a rude comment because his mom didn't have the excuse of being surprised by me. She was just openly against me.

My mom said, "I know it hurts. You can't change that woman, and we can't either. We tried talking to her, but she didn't listen. She's making a big mistake. She's insecure and you shouldn't take it out on yourself. But you have other friends, and other people don't decide who you are as a person. Make sure you're a good person in your heart. And, if you can, forgive her."

It was good advice. I can't say I put a lot of time or thought into forgiving Luke's mom, but I stopped being upset about it, which is almost the same.

Life Is Unfair

NATHANIEL My brother, Jacob, and I are really different, and we fight a lot. In Charlotte, he and his friends played sports—organized games with rules. My friends and I spent all of our free time playing superheroes, where everything came from our imaginations and could change directions anytime. Jacob and his crew saw that we were onto a good thing. They joined in our games, and my mom was glad to see that we were getting along for once. I'm very easy to get along with. So long as I'm the boss.

MAGDA For Jacob's sixth birthday, he really, really wanted to rent a bouncy house with a water slide. He wanted it because he loved water slides. But maybe a tiny part of him suspected his eight-year-old big brother wouldn't be able to participate, and the attention could finally be on him. We were very aware of how Nathaniel's needs affected Jacob's childhood on a daily basis. If ever a sibling could say that his childhood was "unfair," it was Jacob. His whole schedule revolved around Nathaniel's schedule and medical needs. His needs were second.

When Nathaniel had a g-tube and we were stuck in the house, my mother-in-law gave Jacob little pots and pans and measuring cups, and other brightly colored cooking tools. He had a special drawer labeled "Jacob's cooking drawer," and he'd help me blend food for Nathaniel. I told him, "Jacob, you're giving your brother the gift of nutrition." Jacob was enthusiastic about it, but it was not necessarily his first choice. He's a people-pleaser, meaning he tries to make everyone happy. Maybe he was born this way, or maybe he figured out early on that it was the easiest way to deal with his place in our special needs family.

For this birthday party, we decided Jacob should get to choose his birthday activity, regardless of whether it worked for his brother, so we rented an inflatable water slide for the backyard. It hooked up to a garden hose at the top, and water flowed continuously down the side. At the bottom was a pool that filled, eventually flooded, and inevitably destroyed the garden. As far as I could tell, that was the only way to work it.

NATHANIEL I wanted to take a turn on the slide before all the kids arrived and it got too crowded. The pool at the bottom was so shallow that I wouldn't even need someone to catch me. I tightened the cap on my trach, climbed to the top, and let 'er rip. I had literally one second of fun. But the minute I plunged to the bottom, my trach filled with water and my dad had to suction me. My parents said I couldn't to do the water slide again. At the moment, I'm sure I thought that was the worst thing in the world. I'd been anticipating the fun of this water slide, and nobody had said anything about me not being able to do it.

MAGDA This time Nathaniel was upset. There were a handful of times when he was upset that he couldn't do everything the other kids did. We tackled these on a case-by-case basis, deciding when we felt he should accept his lot in life and when we felt he deserved our sympathy.

For example, when all the other kids in the neighborhood started riding bikes, I pushed him to join them. We lived on a safe, long street, and that's what the kids did all summer. Every kid should know how to ride a bike, and I didn't want him to miss out. But Nathaniel wasn't enthusiastic. Part of his resistance had to do with the helmet. It didn't fit over his hearing aid, and yet it wasn't safe (or fun) for him to ride without being able to hear. Russel cut a piece out of the helmet to make room for the hearing aid, but the trach was right in the spot where the strap fastened. Then I bought him a tiny helmet that didn't interfere with the hearing aid, but because of his small chin, the bottom strap kept slipping forward.

As far as Nathaniel was concerned, the solution was easy: he could ride without a helmet. But I wasn't about to let him do that either. His next proposal was to return to his recumbent, three-wheeled bike that was so low to the ground it could be ridden without a helmet, but I wanted him to ride a two-wheeler, to check off that milestone. So I made him wear the annoying, tiny helmet. Since it was unlikely to do any good, I also ran alongside him as he biked, ready to catch him at any moment. Needless to say, wearing a miniature bike helmet while his mother running alongside his bike was not exactly a thrilling scenario for a young boy who just wanted to play with his friends. He'd complain, cry, and call me unfair, but I insisted.

It was the same thing with tying his shoes. He was lazy and refused to tie his shoes. I insisted that Nathaniel learn. I didn't want him to be an adult, on a trip with friends, having to ask someone to tie his shoes because he wanted to play tennis.

We pushed Nathaniel to participate, but we also were sympathetic to the games he couldn't play and the amount of time he spent in doctors' offices, in the hospital, on his way to one of those places, or recovering from another surgery. So one way in which we indulged Nathaniel was by always making sure he had the latest and greatest toys. Whatever his newest passion was—first Thomas & Friends, later Legos and video games—he had every toy that money could buy. I felt like he deserved it. Meanwhile, Jacob didn't get the latest and greatest. I felt guilty about that, but Jacob really didn't mind. He was happy with a baseball mitt and a ball.

On Jacob's sixth birthday, Nathaniel had a fit. He was upset that Jacob got to have a fun party and he couldn't be part of it, screaming "It's not fair. Take that slide back! I don't want it in my yard!"

Then Jacob got upset. It was Jacob's day, and he didn't want his brother's frustration to ruin his party. Because his birthday was in the middle of the summer, and that was when we always scheduled Nathaniel's surgeries, Jacob rarely got to have a real party, and now his big brother was ruining it.

Russel said, "Get this kid out of here. Whatever it takes. Let his brother enjoy himself."

I took Nathaniel to a go-cart track, promising him and Jacob that we'd come back when they were doing the cake. When Nathaniel and I left, Russel went into the house to hide that he was crying because he hated that we couldn't enjoy birthdays like a normal family.

NATHANIEL   It's hard for me to imagine that I ever said anything as bratty as "Take that slide back. I don't want it in my yard." But Jacob and I fought the way brothers do, and then some. My mom really doesn't like it, but she has five siblings to choose from. I have just the one. No options. No trade-ins. No upgrades.

Patient Patience

NATHANIEL   We lived in North Carolina, but I had a new medical team that was in Cincinnati, Ohio. It was a ten-hour drive from Charlotte to Cincinnati, and we went there and back almost once a month. I spent those drives plotting the adventures of a warrior combat team. How else is an eight-year-old kid supposed to survive that much time in a car, going no place new? In my imaginary game, every kid in our neighborhood was a member of this team, and we were tasked with defending the city of Cincinnati against evil powers.

MAGDA   Our doctor at NYU, Dr. Bernstein, had tried around six times to open up Nathaniel's airway without success, so he sent us to Dr. Johnson at Cincinnati Children's Hospital. Our ultimate goal was to create an airway so Nathaniel could breathe through his nose, which was currently blocked by bone. Dr. Johnson and his team took their sweet time mapping out the bone structure of Nathaniel's face. They spent more than a year planning for the surgery. Surgeries. He would have one big surgery first, to open his airway. It was the biggest surgery he'd ever had at that point. If you looked at it from the outside, it seemed so simple. All they wanted to do was to open a pathway in his nose. But the structures in his face were so close together and out of whack compared to a normal person. There was a significant risk of damaging his vision or brain.

NATHANIEL I had no bone where I needed bone, and bone where I wasn't supposed to have bone. I needed surgeries to help grow more bone in my jaw. And I needed surgeries to clear away bone in the back of my nose. It was a cosmic joke that wasn't remotely funny. I only bothered to understand what I had to. Instead of focusing on my medical issues, I came home from those trips and updated my friends on the imaginary universe I was creating for us all. After school, all my friends would come to the house. I'd tell them what their roles and powers were, and announce that there were a few things I needed to teach them in ninja training school. Then we would all run around the neighborhood doing our training exercises.

My mom says it made her happy to see me using my imagination to play with my friends. She remembers playing that way when she was a young girl in Poland.

ZAP! FLASHBACK!

MAGDA My uncle, who was a park ranger in our area, had a big forest behind his house. Every Sunday after church, we'd have a big family lunch at his house, then my brother, sister, cousins, and I would play together for hours. We'd make houses in the woods out of sheets and sticks, climb trees, make mud soups with flower petal spices. Every once in a while, in the evening, we'd make a fire in the backyard and roast kielbasa.

At one of those nighttime gatherings, my uncle said, "I have something to show you guys." By flashlight, he led a parade of us kids into the woods. Coming to an open, grassy area, he pulled aside a nondescript clump of leaves to reveal a mother hedgehog, with a bunch of pink-skinned newborn babies. I was in awe, gazing at the cute babies and realizing how often we ran about among the trees unaware of what creatures were right underfoot. From then on I imagined hidden worlds all around us, their stories waiting to be told.

When I wasn't looking for fairies in the woods behind our house, I read. Among other books, I consumed all forty-seven books in a Scandinavian fantasy series called *The Legend of the Ice People*. (In their witchy culture, every time a child was born, the mom would die. This part only stood out to me when I became a mom.) Anyway, there was a good prince in those books, a hero with superpowers, that I fell in love with. His name was Nathaniel, and that's where I got the idea that one day I would have a son and name him Nathaniel.

MAGDA Now the real boy, the namesake of the books that inspired me, was writing his own legends, using stories to carry him through dull times.

One day I drove Nathaniel to Cincinnati in crazy pouring rain. It was so torrential that I had to wonder if driving in it was a mistake. But the appointment was scheduled, and Russel had taken off work to be with Jacob. I wasn't going to let a lot of rain stop us.

Nathaniel spent the entire ten-plus hours of the drive telling me the story of one single battle. The storm made it hard to see the road ahead—I wanted to focus on driving instead of Nathaniel's story. I was silently praying for a short break—perhaps he'd take a nap—or maybe we could enjoy a quiet musical interlude. But no, only as we finally reached our destination was Cincinnati saved!

The doctor asked if Nathaniel had any questions about the upcoming surgery. I wasn't really surprised when he politely requested that the doctor give him Spiderman fingers at the same time as he worked on his nose.

NATHANIEL The big surgery was scheduled for my winter break from third grade. I thought it would be a much better idea to schedule it during school, not vacation, but nobody seemed to take me seriously.

The day of the surgery finally arrived. We made the same long car trip I was used to and arrived at the same hotel we'd been staying in every time we went to Cincinnati. The best thing about the hotel was that a parrot named Emmy lived in a cage in the lobby! I tried to have conversations with Emmy, who only squawked a lot and said "hello" on a good day.

When it came to surgery, me and my parents were pros. We had it down to a science. As we headed to the pre-op room, we would always pass rooms where other kids were waiting with their parents. They all looked nervous, even if they were there for something small. Meanwhile, our pre-op room was more of a party. Whenever I was going under general anesthesia, my doctors deliberately squeezed in multiple procedures. It was much more efficient that way. If I'd had every surgery separately, I'd never have left the hospital.

Multiple procedures meant multiple doctors, all checking different parts of me before the surgery. So, at any given time, there could be a gastroenterologist, an anesthesiologist, a craniofacial surgeon, a general surgeon, an ENT, a plastic surgeon, and a dental specialist in my room. And nurses and students. There was a line out the door and down the hall. I knew many of them by name, but I couldn't spell some of their jobs if you paid me. My room was like a train station at rush hour. Through all this I just played video games, pausing when someone needed to check my vitals. Parents aren't strict about screen time when you're waiting for surgery, believe me.

Once, when I was little, I had a surgery scheduled for eleven in the morning. You can't eat for eight hours (or drink clear fluids like water or apple juice for five hours) before being put under general anesthesia, so the last meal I'd had was dinner the night before. The surgery was delayed . . . and delayed and delayed. We were waiting in a boring pre-op room and I couldn't eat the whole time. Finally, they told us that the surgery had been rescheduled for four in the afternoon. So not only did we have several more hours to wait in the boring room, but I *still* wasn't allowed to eat. Dad got really mad. I could see that he was about to give the nurses a piece of his mind. I was hungry. For some reason I was craving Indian food. But I figured if there was a delay, there was probably a good reason. I was pretty sure the doctor wasn't sitting in an ice cream parlor having trouble deciding which flavor he wanted to order.

I said, "Dad, if the doctors are late, there is probably a little boy in the operating room that needs them more than me. I'm fine, Daddy, we can wait."

Then my dad felt bad and said, "I know, you're right." He probably cried. You know, because he thought I was being a compassionate child. The truth is I just didn't want him to make a scene.

Once I have the gown on for surgery, I get a weird feeling, cold and weak, as if my body is preparing to shut down. On the way to the OR for some reason my legs feel like toothpicks and I can't stand on them. That's why my dad always carries me.

MAGDA Every time Nathaniel has had surgery, from the time he was a baby, Russel gets into a gown and carries him into the OR. The hospital might have fourteen operating rooms, and Nathaniel is inevitably in the one at the end of a long hallway. Russel swears that, as he walks, the hallway gets longer. Carrying Nathaniel all that way, Russel breaks a sweat. In Russel's arms, Nathaniel goofs around, which helps him get through it, but he never ever resists or makes a fuss.

NATHANIEL It's always the same. The OR is a big room, all cold metal and machines. There's a viewing balcony and giant flat-screen TVs with images of my skeleton. There are huge lights, and white sheets draped over the trays of knives and scissors. I guess they don't want me to see the tools they'll be using to have at me. There might be six to ten medical professionals in scrubs, playing with knobs on various machines. Once we're in the operating room, Dad sits on the table with me on his lap, ready to attach the gas tube to my trach. The gas is what puts me to sleep for the surgery, and I'm always nervous to take it. It doesn't hurt, but knowing I'm being put under makes me feel kind of sick, so that's when I bring out my best delay tactics. I ask every doctor in the room about their roles, what all the machines are, why there are pink beads in the anesthesia machine, and so on. I'm at my most inquisitive when I'm stalling. Dad lets me hold things up for a bit, but eventually I take a deep breath and tell him I'm ready.

MAGDA The doctors are taught to watch for physical phases as the anesthetic knocks the patient out. I'm never in the OR, but Russel tells me that the anesthesiologists always get a kick out of Nathaniel's narration of his own condition. He walks them through every phase they are looking for. "My voice is starting to change. My muscles are starting to feel stiff."

The anesthesiologist turns to Russel and says, "He's giving me the play-by-play!"

NATHANIEL When they start the gas, I feel fine, and then it kicks in all at once. I know that in five more seconds it will ram me.

Sounds start morphing from echo-y to robotic.

It's almost like I'm watching a video of me talking— I know what I'm saying but can't quite control it.

Then Dad's hands feel clammy.

Then I start feeling like it's not happening.

Then I get really dizzy and start to slur my words.

Then I fall asleep.

MÁGDA Once Nathaniel is unconscious, Russel lays him down, takes off his hearing aid, walks out, and collapses. But I only know this because Russel has told me. By the time he gets back to the family waiting room, I am already completely out. It doesn't matter how small or uncomfortable the chair is, I fall dead asleep the minute Russel carries Nathaniel away. Sleeping is how I deal with stress, and for the most part it's a good coping strategy—it's hard to show weakness when you're asleep! So that's what I do. I don't get up to eat. I don't need to go to the bathroom. No matter how long the surgery lasts, there I am, covered in blankets, sleeping through the entire thing until Russel shakes me and says the doctor is on his way to tell us how it went.

NATHANIEL I always wake up from surgery angry. It must be a side effect of the anesthesia. Of course, I can't hear because they've taken out my hearing aid, and I've never liked that. But instead of politely asking for it back, I'm full of rage. Once I punched a nurse who tried to hold my hand. I've been known to try to rip out an IV, the skinny tube through which they give me fluids and medications. Even though I always have to stay in the hospital to recover, and I know this, I still wake up saying, "I just want to go home. I don't want to be here anymore." I'm loopy from drugs, in pain, and crusty with blood. People are saying "Hi Nathaniel, hi Nathaniel," and it feels like they're not giving me time to wake up. Five minutes later I've calmed down and am ready to move from the recovery room to a hospital room, usually on a different floor.

MAGDA The doctors in Cincinnati had prepared for months to open Nathaniel's nose, and at the end of the eighteen-hour surgery, they were successful. We had a little hope that getting Nathaniel's nose open would mean we could take the trach out, but we all knew it wasn't likely. The long surgery didn't allow Nathaniel to get rid of his trach, but it set him on the path. His nose was open and his breathing was improved, but his airway was still not big enough. Even so, there was now a light at the end of the tunnel. The doctor promised us it was the first step of a long journey, and still cause for celebration.

We returned to Cincinnati, first every four weeks, then at longer intervals for Nathaniel to have eight to ten smaller follow-up surgeries. The doctors repeatedly cleared away the scar tissue, which was so eager to close the hole that the doctors had created. At our final appointment in Cincinnati, Dr. Johnson, who had operated on Nathaniel so many times, said, "I have some news to share. I'm moving to Seattle Children's hospital." We thought that meant that whenever Nathaniel had his next surgery, Dr. Johnson wouldn't be part of it. Little did we know that three years later this doctor would again become a huge part of our lives.

PART III

WONDER

A "Real-Life" Auggie

NATHANIEL Four years before our first meeting with Dr. Hopper, in February 2012, when I was eight, the book *Wonder* by R.J. Palacio was published. *Wonder*, which millions of kids all over the world have now read, is the story of a boy named Auggie Pullman. Auggie has a craniofacial condition. It's called mandibulofacial dysostosis in the book, which is a harder-to-say name for Treacher Collins, the same disorder that I have.

The book begins when, after having been homeschooled while he had lots of surgeries, Auggie goes to his neighborhood school for the first time in fifth grade.

MAGDA *Wonder* focuses on the challenges Auggie faces interacting with the people around him at the new school, some of whom are uncomfortable around him. Told from Auggie's perspective and that of some of the people in his life, the book is funny and moving and real.

Auggie won the hearts of readers, and it's not an exaggeration to say that it taught a whole generation of children, and many to follow, to accept others who look different. To choose kindness.

Wonder had a huge effect on our lives. It didn't change how Nathaniel saw himself, but it immediately changed the way people saw and approached him in playgrounds, at school, in the world. *Wonder* introduced the rest of the world to some of the things Nathaniel had dealt with his whole life. In doing so, it gave readers true empathy for real people living with facial differences—with *any* differences!

Nathaniel and Auggie have a lot of the same physical issues, but they are not exactly the same. For one thing, Nathaniel is real and Auggie is fictional. Also, how the kids at school react to his appearance is very upsetting to Auggie. People assume that the same is true for Nathaniel. And yes, how people treat Nathaniel, how people see him, what he *looks like* does matter—probably to me as his mother more than to him—but when it came to Nathaniel's problems, his appearance wasn't a priority for any of us. It wasn't even on the list! He was dealing with such major physical challenges—breathing!—on a daily basis, we simply didn't have the time and energy to worry about whether Nathaniel looked "normal" or whether people treated him differently. We had bigger fish to fry.

NATHANIEL My dad ordered a copy of the book *Wonder* soon after it came out. He heard about it from other parents in the craniofacial community. Dad doesn't read books a lot. He mostly reads the newspaper. But when he started reading *Wonder*, he didn't stop. He read parts of it out loud to the whole family, crying the whole time. I don't love to read, but I read *Wonder* a couple of times. I didn't think about myself so much, but I really cared about Auggie.

MAGDA The first time Russel read the book *Wonder*, he finished it in one day. I tried to start the book, but the truth is that I picked it up, read a few pages, and said, "I can't read this right now." Because right away I felt a surge of self-pity, and pity for myself and from others is a feeling I really don't like. I avoid it at all costs. The book reminded me too much of my own life. It hit too close to home.

Russel sped through it, though, and he found the similarities to our lives uncanny. It felt like the author knew our lives. Russel immediately called our friend Nurse Pat to talk to her about this amazing book.

Pat said, "Are you kidding? The author is sitting in the room with me right this minute." Apparently, when R.J. was researching the book, she had visited the medical center to meet with experts on the syndrome. The first thing she saw when she walked in the front door was a huge picture of Nathaniel hanging on the wall, so she'd known a bit about Nathaniel for a long time. Right after that phone call, Pat put R.J. and Russel in touch.

Sometime after that phone call, when we were in New York to see doctors, Russel and I met R.J. at a cute café in New York's West Village. She told us about the event that inspired her to write the book: she and her kids had gone into an ice cream store in Brooklyn and had seen a child with Treacher Collins. Her younger child had a bad reaction—he was scared or upset. Unsure how to handle the situation, she hurried them away from the store.

I figured out immediately that the child they saw at the ice cream parlor was Emily. "I know that family,"

I said. "I know Emily and her mother, Jenna. Jenna helped me cope when I was first digesting Nathaniel's condition as a baby. She's the most amazing person I've ever met."

I told R.J. that her child's response was understandable. It had even been hard for me to meet Emily. This is horrible to say and disturbing to me, but I almost fainted when I saw my friend Jenna's daughter for the first time. Emily didn't have a trach, but her features were small and fragile and close together and shocking. How silly and embarrassing this is, but I admit it. I admit it because it is important for all of us to acknowledge that, no matter how kind and fair we want to be, sometimes we still have reactions that we can't control. Even me.

I'm definitely not perfect, but I'm honest about my imperfections because I hope it helps people understand themselves and each other. Even now, after all I have experienced, I might still have that reaction. It says nothing about Emily and everything about me. The point is, if I can have this reaction, the loving and experienced mother of a boy with Treacher Collins, then anyone can. The best we can do is try to manage it with grace.

I told R.J. all this, but she said, "I'm still not okay with my reaction. It wasn't my child's fault. I was the one who pulled him away." Her own way of handling the situation haunted her. "I couldn't let go of what I'd done," she told me. "I felt like I owed this mother and this girl an apology, so I wrote it in the form of the book."

I liked R.J's style. Talking to me, the mother of a son with the same condition, she didn't make excuses. She took responsibility for her actions as a mother. Sure, her hurried flight from the ice cream store hadn't been ideal, but it wasn't anything new to me. I saw it all the time, the shocked faces of people, their unfiltered reactions. Finally, one of them had done something about it! Her warmth and kindness were captivating. She was humble, honest, and pure. She herself wanted to change, and by writing *Wonder* she did something to help millions of people change. It was beautiful.

At that time *Wonder* had just been published, and R.J. told us that so far it had sold 1,600 copies, not an enormous number. She was giving presentations at schools and libraries, trying to spread her message through the story. In her meetings with the students, they were very curious about what Auggie looked like. R.J., remembering the photo that she'd seen of Nathaniel when she first walked into the hospital, told us that his image was in her head when she created Auggie.

Even so, R.J. was struck when we told her how many details of our lives she'd captured in the book without ever meeting us. Later, when Nathaniel started making appearances at schools and other places with her, she would say, "Nathaniel Newman is Auggie Pullman come to life." But in the beginning, when we first met R.J., we had no idea that so many people would come to know and love Auggie Pullman as a character. We couldn't imagine how important the book would be to us, to the craniofacial community, and to a whole generation of kids.

NATHANIEL A year after my parents first met R.J., when I was in fourth grade, we moved to New Jersey for my dad's job. (I know, my dad changed jobs a lot.) By then *Wonder* was very popular, and R.J. was visiting lots of schools. Now that we lived nearby, R.J. contacted us and said, "I'm going to visit a private school on the Upper West Side of Manhattan. Do you think you could join me?" She thought it would be helpful for the kids to meet someone like Auggie and put a face to the character.

It may sound strange, but even though I loved *Wonder*, I didn't take it personally. In fact, Jacob had a bigger reaction to *Wonder* than I did. He was in second grade when he read the book for the first time, and he read it all in one sitting. Jacob was excited by the similarities between me and Auggie: how Auggie, like me, had one true friend instead of lots of friends. And how we both loved *Star Wars*. And our dogs. How Auggie struggled with everyday things: eating, making friends, being in dusty situations, not being able to swim.

Where Jacob saw the similarities, I tended to see the differences. People expect me to identify with Auggie, and get all emotional, and cry like my dad. But to me, though Auggie has medical issues that are similar to mine, he has a completely different personality.

In many ways my life was nothing like Auggie's. The biggest difference was how self-conscious Auggie was about his face. He often wore a space helmet to hide it, and Halloween was his favorite holiday because when he wore a mask he felt and was treated just like everyone else. As for me, I never wanted to hide on Halloween. I loved it because I got to be a superhero, just like any other superhero-loving kid. Also, kids were never as mean to me as they are to Auggie in the book. Nobody drew pictures saying I looked like Freddy Krueger from the horror movie *A*

Nightmare on Elm Street, and nobody ever told me that I should kill myself!

MAGDA The comments other kids made to Nathaniel weren't as extreme as they are in *Wonder,* and the things they did say rarely bothered Nathaniel. So far, at fifteen, Nathaniel still has never felt like he didn't want to show his face.

It sounds a little funny to say, but Nathaniel seems naturally well-suited to the challenges he was given. He walks through life only seeing the bright side. If someone is standing on the sidewalk cursing, and another person is walking a puppy, he only sees the puppy. When he was younger and his differences were more apparent, he barely noticed the stares and double-takes when people first saw him—he'd gotten them his whole life—and if somebody said something mean, such as, "His face is weird," he might have given them a look, but he'd keep walking, unbothered.

In New York hospitals, when Nathaniel arrived for surgery, the nurse always checked his vitals and went through a list of questions to see if he was in good shape for surgery. When he got to be a certain age, they added a series of questions about his home life. Things like: Is anyone touching you inappropriately at home? At school? Do you ever think about suicide? They ask the parents to step out of the room for this part so the child feels safe telling the authorities if his parents are treating him badly.

When he was around eight or nine, he was in the prep room being asked these questions. After the nurse was finished, she came out crying.

"What did he do? What happened?" I asked.

The nurse, who knew what we'd been through, said, "I asked him one of the questions: Have you ever thought about hurting yourself?

"Nathaniel said, 'That might be the stupidest question I've heard in my life.'

"I said, 'What do you mean?'

"And he said, 'I have the greatest life ever. I have an awesome mom and dad and brother. I have a dog named Smokey. Why would I hurt myself? My life is awesome.'"

Then I understood that the nurse wasn't upset. She was moved by his optimistic way of seeing the world.

Jacob seems to be wired differently from his brother. He says that if he had Treacher Collins and looked like Nathaniel, the curious toddlers would have made him mad or sad. He is sure that in Nathaniel's shoes, he would have a panic attack before every surgery. And he thinks that after a while he would get so tired of it that he'd verbally and physically attack people. He doesn't think he's as mentally strong as Nathaniel—in a lacrosse game he gets really upset when things don't go his way. (It's something he's working on.) But we'll never know if Nathaniel was born equipped to deal with his challenges, or whether he simply rose to meet them because he had to.

NATHANIEL When I did the first school visit with R.J., I sat in the front of the stage with my mom, Jacob, and R.J. Her husband was in the audience. The fourth-grade class gathered in front of us—they had already read the book for school and were there to meet a "real-life Auggie." I didn't know what questions to expect, but a lot of kids asked, "Does it hurt? Were you in a fire? What happened to you?" One kid asked, "Are you in a special class for special kids?"

I don't mind when people ask how I acquired these facial features, although ideally they could put the question aside and just get to know me. What I really don't like is when the questions jump to assumptions. Being asked if I was in a fire, or if I'm in a special class for special kids rubs me the wrong way. It's like saying, "Hi, nice to meet you. Have you ever fallen down a hole?" Or "Why is your hair brown?" I don't spend time wondering, much less asking, why someone looks a particular way. There's an answer, but does it need to be known? It doesn't matter and it's not my business.

MAGDA It's hard for me to remember how I used to talk to people with visible disabilities before Nathaniel was born, but now I am completely open and maybe even too friendly because of the connection I feel with them. Once, when I was working in a store, I met a temporary employee, a young guy with a huge scar across his face. I said, "I know we just met, but do you mind explaining what happened to you?"

He smiled immediately and said, "Oh my gosh, you are the first person who has actually asked. There's a story behind this scar, but if nobody asks, I never get a chance to tell it. I was in a terrible car accident. I'm happy to be alive, and my scar is a reminder of how lucky I am."

Of course, not everyone is always in the mood to talk, and it's not their responsibility to answer my questions. But having Nathaniel taught me that one thing is certain: it's better to ask than to stare or be rude.

NATHANIEL I visited schools to support R.J. and the book because it was kind of fun, but in my day-to-day life I don't want to be seen as Auggie Pullman, or "the real *Wonder* boy." First of all, I'm not the only kid with Treacher Collins, and second, I just want to be seen as Nathaniel Newman. I want to be seen as a normal kid who happens to look different.

Nonetheless, I like the message people take away from the book. I understand how powerful *Wonder* is, and what it is doing to help us all relate to each other.

A Dog. And Another Dog.
And Another Dog.

NATHANIEL In New Jersey, my mom took a job during the holiday rush working part-time at a store that sells workout clothes. Our dog Smokey was two years old (and I was nine).

Smokey was our first dog, a cockapoo. Back when we lived in North Carolina, we saw an ad for puppies on the side of the road in the Blue Ridge mountains near my grandparents' house, two hours away from us in Hendersonville, North Carolina. There were two eleven-week-old puppies left, and Smokey tried to bite the top of my shoes in a friendly way.

We brought Smokey home, and he became our neighborhood's favorite dog. He loved waking us up for school every day—he loved it so much that he did on the weekends too. And then he walked with us to school.

In New Jersey, with the whole family at work and school all day long, Smokey got lonely. He'd never been alone for such long stretches of time. Every day as my mom drove away from the house, she'd see Smokey watching from the bay window, looking like he thought none of his family would ever return. When we came home, he was still in the window, waiting. Poor Smokey needed a friend.

MÁGDA We needed another hypoallergenic dog—fur and trachs don't mix—and online I found a place in Pennsylvania Amish country where they advertised cockapoo puppies. At the time, I didn't know anything about the puppy mills—breeding operations where all they care about is making money and the puppies are treated inhumanely.

We drove three hours to the address I'd been given and came to an oddly empty house. It was clear that nobody lived there. Then a man appeared. Acting as if this were his home, he mentioned his wife and children, and said that everyone was working, but something was off. Only later would I realize that he'd probably had us meet him there instead of at a huge, filthy warehouse stuffed with hundreds of dogs.

Nonetheless, he went into the empty house and returned with two cute puppies, releasing them to tumble and jump on the grass. He picked one up. "This is yours."

This was definitely not the dog I'd seen in the picture online, a cockapoo named "Monica." This was a mixed breed dog. A shedding dog. Possibly a golden retriever–Chihuahua mix.

Russel said, "That's not a cockapoo."

The guy said, "You don't want it, leave."

But it was too late. The boys were already fawning over the dog.

Coco was sweet and good, and Smokey loved her. She was the first female dog we'd had, and the boys treated her like their baby, dressing her in pink tutus and choosing pink plushies for her at the pet store. She even had a pink bed. We'd never had pink around the house. Now we had a spoiled baby girl.

Every day we walked to school with the two dogs. The boys' classmates would pet Coco and say, "She's so cute! What kind of dog is she?" We told them she was an Amish cockapoo.

Smokey still sat at the bay window waiting for us to come home, but now Coco was right there next to him and the mournful look was gone from Smokey's eyes.

NATHANIEL Coco walked to school with us every day. Dogs weren't allowed on the school grounds, but my mom bought them service dog bandanas to wear around their necks. One said "Smokey the Service Dog" and the other said "Coco the Service Dog." She says it's the only time she exploited my disability.

We only had Coco for a year. We moved to Reno, Nevada for my dad's job and I started fifth grade there. On the day Coco turned one, we dressed her in a colorful tutu and she walked proudly to the school. The other kids loved her, and we told everyone, "It's Coco's birthday." That was a Friday. The next day was Saturday. I remember like it was yesterday. We were in our rental apartment. Jacob and I were home, Mom was at yoga, and Dad went to take Smokey and Coco on a walk. Just after they left, I heard a noise. The door opened and Dad yelled "Get my keys! Coco got hit by a car!" Moments later, Dad started to drive away, but he didn't even get to the end of the driveway before he stopped. He came back inside, carrying Coco in his arms, and said, "She's in heaven." It was a tragedy. She turned one on Friday and was gone on Saturday.

Smokey went to her as if he knew something was wrong. He licked her, trying to wake her up.

We had to call Mom and tell her. I could hear her crying on the other end of the line. She came home and took me to a shelter to try to find a replacement for Coco. The same day she died! Mom wasn't really thinking straight. At the shelter, she started looking for another dog that looked exactly like Coco, but it was really like she was hoping to find Coco herself. Like I said, Mom was kind of hysterical. I watched her cry and thought, *I have to make sure she doesn't get a dog.*

I tried to comfort her, saying, "Coco's in heaven now, let's just go home."

Meanwhile she was saying, "This dog shakes his tail just like Coco, the eyes look like Coco, the coloring." We spent about two hours there, searching hopelessly.

Then my mom went to the front desk and said, "Are there more dogs? I'm looking for my dog." She described Coco, and the rescue workers clearly thought she was actually looking for a lost dog, because they took us from the adoption side of the shelter to the other side, where they had dogs who had been found on the street and weren't yet up for adoption. My mom fell in love with a pair of Brittanys who looked a lot like Coco.

Finally, I said, "Please, let's go home," and dragged her out of there.

MAGDA The boys had never experienced death before, and they had different reactions to the loss of Coco. Jacob talked about her often, and when Russel took them to a crafting program at a children's museum in Reno, Jacob made a blue pillow with buttons on it and wrote "Coco" on it with a Sharpie. He slept with that pillow every night. Once, when the other dogs (soon to join the family) got ahold of the Coco pillow and made a hole in it, Jacob was as upset as he'd been when she died. I found a sewing kit and fixed it on the spot. From then on Jacob kept the Coco pillow hidden under his regular pillow.

Nathaniel didn't talk about Coco much, but he would look at pictures of her and feel sad. Together, we read a poem about a pet crossing a rainbow bridge into a beautiful meadow where he would frolic until his owner joined him. Nathaniel seemed to take that story to heart. In his mind, Coco was up in heaven, waiting for him.

When I recovered my senses, we found another dog, Snowball, at a puppy store in Nevada. I told them both to think of it as though Coco's sacrifice brought us Snowball, (and then Brownie, and then Coda).

After surgeries, Snowball seemed to know better than I how to help Nathaniel heal. Every night, when he went to bed, Snowball got under his covers and waited until Nathaniel fell asleep. Then she came out to let me know that her work there was done, and now she was ready to comfort me.

Hollywood

NATHANIEL When *Wonder* became a bestseller, something changed. In parks and playgrounds and on the street, instead of staring at me, people started to ask, "Oh, have you read *Wonder*? You look like the boy from the *Wonder* book." People were starting to understand my face better.

My mom or I would answer, "We did read the book and we know the author."

MAGDA These seemingly trivial exchanges with strangers were a small change and a big one. Part of why seeing Nathaniel for the first time made people uncomfortable was that they didn't know what they were seeing. What was going on with this kid? Was he okay? What should they think of him? How should they react? They didn't know what questions to ask in order to understand him. Maybe things changed because they had a picture of Auggie in their heads after reading the book, or maybe just seeing a boy whose face was different sparked the connection. Either way, it was to *Wonder*'s credit. Practically overnight, the book gave a lot of kids a way to process Nathaniel's face and the idea that there was a real, likeable person behind it.

Obviously, this wasn't just about Nathaniel. It was true for other kids with Treacher Collins, and anybody with a craniofacial condition. It turned out that brilliant blue book and its message was all they'd ever needed. Nathaniel still got stares, but not as often as when he was a little child, and these stares were different. Kids were curious, but they did not react and run away. Parents were willing to come up to us and ask questions.

NATHANIEL I like when people are better educated and don't say stuff just to say it, but I'm not angry or hurt when people are rude or ignorant. In Auggie's world, school is new territory, a place where he has to cope with kids who don't know how to handle him. Maybe part of what makes me different from him (other than that he is fictional and I am real) is that Auggie is going to school and dealing with his classmates for the first time in fifth grade. I started school in kindergarten, so I experienced my classmates' reactions from the age of six.

In Reno, when my dad and I wrote the letter introducing me to my new classmates, it said, "You've probably read the book *Wonder*. That book is about a boy who is just like me."

Wonder didn't change what I thought when I saw other people. It didn't change me. But it changed how other people approached me practically overnight, and, in that way, it changed my life. *Wonder* made the world feel like a friendlier place.

MAGDA   Around Thanksgiving of 2014, just before we left New Jersey for Reno, Russel and R.J. talked. She told him some good news: there was going to be a movie of *Wonder*! It would be cool to see the book and syndrome we knew so well come to life on the big screen. Also, R.J.'s message—choose kindness—would reach an even wider audience. They already had a director and a screenwriter, and R.J. told us that she had proposed that Nathaniel play Auggie.

"He's my real-life Auggie," she said. "That's how I picture Auggie."

The producers flew Nathaniel from Reno to Los Angeles and gave him a script with a couple of scenes to practice.

NATHANIEL   When my parents asked me if I'd like to try out for the movie, I said, "Will I miss school?"

They said I would.

"Sounds good," I told them.

So my parents made arrangements for me to audition. In Los Angeles! For a Hollywood movie! The audition was kind of like taking a test. I memorized my lines. I tried to put feeling into it without overacting or underacting. But I'm pretty sure I'm not the best actor. I can role-play with my friend Andy, but that's improvisation. It's not the same as taking someone else's words and character and making them come to life.

One of the scenes took place on Halloween when Auggie is upset about something that happened at school and tells his sister he doesn't want to go trick-or-treating. In another scene Auggie is talking too loudly and gets kicked out of the library. (I don't think that scene ended up in the movie.) At one point in the audition, I got confused. The woman playing the librarian told me to leave. I wasn't prepared for that—I didn't know if she was saying her line, or if she really wanted me to get off the stage. I figured they didn't actually want me to leave the audition, so at first I just stood there. Then she told me to leave again, this time more harshly, so I walked out of the room. As I left she said, "Where are you going?" Yeah, I wasn't a pro.

At the end of the audition, the producers hugged me and told me I did great. I knew they were just being nice. When we left, they told us that they liked the idea of having a kid with Treacher Collins play the part, but they were also looking at professional actors. They asked us to wait, and we'd hear from them. That was fine with me—I didn't know whether to want the part or not.

MÁGDA The movie producers weren't the only people who were interested in Nathaniel's similarities to Auggie. Two years had passed since Nathaniel first visited schools with R.J., and *Wonder* was now being taught in schools nationwide. It had quickly become a phenomenon. All over the country, kids with facial differences were starting to call themselves "*Wonder* kids." Nathaniel was eleven years old. At Nathaniel's new school in Reno, his teacher told someone in her book group that she had "a *Wonder* kid" in her class. Word spread from there to Elizabeth Vargas, a host on a news show called *20/20*. Elizabeth was interested in doing a TV interview with our family about Nathaniel.

We met Elizabeth, and she told us she wanted to explore a part of our story that wasn't central to *Wonder*: the challenge of giving a kid with severe differences the opportunity to have a normal life. We liked what she had to say, and agreed to participate. We'd done something like this before: a short documentary for the National Geographic show *Taboo*. All of us assumed that *20/20* would film something similar. A "slice of life" profile that could be timed with the release of the *Wonder* movie. Which is what they would have done . . . if our lives hadn't taken such an unexpected turn.

PART IV
THE BIG ONE

Dr. Hopper's Surgery

NATHANIEL When we moved to Reno, we started to take trips to Seattle to meet with Dr. Hopper, the doctor whose new surgery might let him close up my tracheostomy. When my first surgeon, Dr. McCarthy, retired, my dad asked him, "Where would you bring your grandson if he had Treacher Collins?" Dr. McCarthy said, "Dr. Hopper at Seattle Children's hospital."

The trach was my Achilles' heel. I always had to be careful with it. I had to keep it safer than the rest of my body. And it was high maintenance. And I couldn't go swimming. Or the doctors *told me* I couldn't swim. In Reno, at the neighborhood pool, I decided I would find a way to go under water. I pushed the trach back and tightened the cap as tight as I could. *I'm gonna try this*, I thought.

"Dad," I said, "I'm going under water."

Dad said, "You gotta risk it to get a biscuit."

My mom isn't quite as open to breaking the rules. She'll say, "You shouldn't do that," and she'll watch, worried, ready to jump in and save me, but she doesn't go so far as to make me stop.

So I ducked my head under. It was only for a second, but when I came up, I was like, *Yeah, I did it! Whoa!* I felt happy and proud. I was being brave. I didn't care what the doctor might say . . . as long as he didn't know.

I said, "Dad, I just went under water and I was fine."

"You did?" he said. Then I showed him.

Even though I could only do it for a second, I liked being underwater better than being above it. I ducked beneath the surface over and over again. The only downside of this version of swimming was that it didn't really work. I couldn't stay under more than a second. Plus, water got into my trach once or twice when the band didn't stay as tight as it needed to be. Also, this act of bravery guaranteed that I would need to change my trach tie because it would get soggy. So, yeah, the reality was that I still couldn't go underwater. But at least I knew I had tried and gone as far as I possibly could.

There was only one way I knew of that I could go further: Dr. Hopper's surgery. That's right, the "draconian" surgery that would take a year from beginning to end and change the shape of my entire face. After all the surgeries I'd had already, what was Dr. Hopper doing that was so big and complicated and exciting? There were a few things he wanted to accomplish in the surgery, but the main point—the huge, life-changing goal of the Big One—was to close up my tracheostomy, that hole in my neck that helped me breathe but also made everything more complicated.

I was on board with trying Dr. Hopper's surgery. I would have to be brave, braver than putting my head under water for a second or two. I know I said surgeries don't feel like acts of bravery because I'm just lying there, asleep, while doctors work on me. The same is true for the big ones, but just the *idea* of them takes some bravery.

MAGDA Dr. Hopper's proposal was incredibly appealing, but it was a big decision. The doctor had explained to us that after the surgery, which would take place in Seattle at the hospital where the doctor was based, Nathaniel would have a heavy framework (we called it the "halo" or the "cage") around his head holding sixteen screws that would be mounted on his skull in various places. Five of those screws needed to be turned one or two millimeters every day. If that doesn't sound bad enough, imagine this: Nathaniel would wake up from surgery with his eyes sewn shut, his jaws wired closed, a feeding tube connected to his stomach, the halo on his head, and he would face *six months* of wearing that cumbersome halo and staying mostly in bed. In the beginning he wouldn't be able to eat or see or talk, which pretty much eliminated every way a bedridden person might keep himself sane for the long weeks of recovery. Would it be too much for Nathaniel to bear?

NATHANIEL Dr. Hopper had performed the surgery he wanted to try on me on two people so far. One was a baby, and one was an eleven-year-old girl named Izzy. One time, when we were at the hospital in Seattle to meet with some of the doctors, Dr. Hopper told us that Izzy and her family were also in the hospital for an appointment. He said, "Let me ask them if they're willing to talk to you guys. When you go to lunch, I'll text you."

But when we stepped out of his office, there she was, with her parents, in the waiting room. Izzy had the cage on her head. It looked . . . draconian. She couldn't talk, but she seemed cheerful enough.

My dad introduced me and told her that I was going to have the same surgery that she'd had.

The family was really nice, and reassuring. Her mom told my mom, "This is the hardest thing we've ever done, but I think it's going to work." Izzy's breathing had already improved. A few weeks after that day, my parents told me that Dr. Hopper had helped with her trach removal. The surgery was a success! Izzy, who had used a g-tube her whole life, was now eating food. Hearing this made me feel a little less nervous about the surgery. If I was going to go through that torture, I really wanted it to work.

A kid like me, with sixty-plus surgeries under my belt before I turned fifteen, is not "normal." And I guess you could say that the goal of all those surgeries was to make me normal. To help me breathe through my nose, eat through my mouth, close my eyes properly, hear without ears. To go to school without a nurse. To play without being careful of the trach. To shower without being helped by my mother (ugh). To speak more clearly. To swim. My parents and the doctors and I all agreed that we wanted me to be able to do those things effortlessly, or with as little effort as possible, like "normal" people.

But even if and when we succeeded, would I be normal then? I'd still be a kid who had more surgeries than most other people. I'd still look a little different, if you care about those things.

Where is the line between normal and not normal?

Who gets to draw that line?

I didn't need people to see me as "normal," but I liked the idea that people might not be so distracted by my face that it was all they thought about when they met me. Without that distraction, it would be easier for them to know the real me. But when Dr. Hopper said the surgery would change my face, I said, "Okay, but not too much. I want my dogs to recognize me."

We decided to do it. The surgery wouldn't change who I was. But it would make living more comfortable. That sounded pretty good.

In preparation for the big surgery, we started flying up to Seattle every two to three months for testing and procedures. They took molds of my mouth, which tasted gross. They made a mask of my face. And they made a 3D replica of my skull so they could figure out how exactly they would do the surgery.

My parents scheduled the surgery for March 2016 expecting a tough three months, at least, to follow. I would miss the end of sixth grade but might be recovered in time to start seventh grade with the rest of my class.

Meanwhile, the movie people had left open the possibility that I would play Auggie. We knew it was highly unlikely, but my mom still wanted to make sure they weren't counting on us. One day, when my mom was walking the dogs, she called one of the producers, Todd Lieberman.

MAGDA I said, "I realize that you're putting a lot of money into this movie, and your schedule doesn't revolve around one boy, but I don't live in your world. I'm just a mom, and I wanted to let you know that we're scheduling a surgery that will change Nathaniel's life. It'd be amazing if Nathaniel or another kid with Treacher Collins could play this role. It would be authentic, and it would bring great exposure to the craniofacial community. We're here to help if there's anything we can do, but this is our priority."

Todd thanked me and told me the movie was already moving ahead. He said, "We have someone in mind for the role."

A couple of days later Todd called Russel. He said, "We got Jacob Tremblay to play the role of Auggie! He's a great actor."

That weekend, Russel and I watched a movie that Jacob had starred in. During the movie we kept looking at each other, saying, "Wow. This kid is amazing. He'll be so awesome playing Auggie." We were blown away.

The next time I talked to Todd I told him he'd made a wise decision. Sure, it would have been great to give the role to someone with a craniofacial condition instead of a "normal" person wearing a mask. But their goal was to make an amazing movie, and the more successful they were, the bigger a spotlight would shine not just on the craniofacial community, but on R.J.'s universal message of accepting difference and choosing kindness.

NATHANIEL I didn't have strong feelings about whether a kid with facial difference had to play the role of Auggie. I thought it would be great either way. The point was to have the best actor, no matter what.

And the reality is that most kids with Treacher Collins don't have a lot of time to develop their acting skills.

MAGDA Meanwhile the *20/20* crew was spending time with our family. We felt honored to represent the community. The film crew went with Nathaniel to the playground. They came hiking with us and the dogs. And they spent time at our house, watching our daily routine. We got so used to having them around that they felt like friends. We kind of missed them when they weren't there.

When we first started the *20/20* project, a year and a half earlier, we were only beginning to explore the possibility of having the halo surgery. The only plan at that point was to talk about the *Wonder* movie release and to show a kid who had a similar life. But now it morphed into: *Wow, this major surgery is insane!* Instead of finishing up their interviewing with us before the surgery, *20/20* decided to make it a more in-depth story, following our family for a couple of *years,* leading up to and including Nathaniel's big surgery. In an odd coincidence, going through the preparation, surgery, and recovery, would take about as long as it took the movie people to make and release *Wonder.*

Good-byes

NATHANIEL My Reno classmates had a get-together to say good-bye to me before I left school. At a certain point they were talking about homework that would be due after I left. I felt kind of smug, but then they started talking about what they were going to do during the summer and in my head I was like, *Have fun with that.*

To get ready for the surgery, Mom took me to a hairdresser to get my head shaved. We figured they'd do a better job than the hospital. Jacob shaved his head to support me—he didn't have to, but I appreciated that he did. It was supposed to be kind of a fun thing, but I was crying on the inside. My precious locks were gone. I do not look good with a shaved head. My 'fro is my trademark.

Mom packed my clothes—after the surgery I would only be able to wear button-down shirts and pajamas for a long time. Nothing that went over the head. And I picked out games to bring with me. I was bringing a mini-TV from GameStop that functioned as a portable game console. I planned to give it hours of action. I also brought an LCD writing tablet. It was sort of like an Etch A Sketch that I would use to communicate when my mouth was wired shut.

The last thing I did before we left for Seattle was to say good-bye to Jacob and the dogs.

MÁGDA By the time Nathaniel was getting ready for the Big Surgery, we had three dogs. My youngest brother, Michal, the one I helped raise, took a month-long break from school to come from Poland and take care of them. Jacob would go on a cruise with his aunt Nancy while Russel and I went to Seattle to see Nathaniel through the surgery.

I wanted to do something fun with Michal before we left, so I booked the two of us on a hot air balloon flight over Napa. The hot air balloon was a thank-you to Michal, but it was also a distraction for me. Nathaniel was calm. I was the one freaking out, and as the mom I was supposed to be sane, or pretend to be sane, because he'd need me. I was scared of heights, but surgery was much scarier. As it happened, the balloon crash-landed onto a tree in some guy's junkyard, and they had to pull us down with ropes. If there was a lesson in that, I have no idea what it was.

A Moment of Terror

NATHANIEL In Seattle, the night before the surgery, I was allowed to eat whatever I wanted. It would be the last meal I tasted for four months. Four months! We went to an Italian restaurant and I ordered a big plate of fettuccine Alfredo and a huge piece of cheesecake. Our appointment at the hospital was at six the next morning.

MÁGDA It was March 22, 2016. The Big Surgery started at 8:00 a.m. and lasted more than eleven hours. Nathaniel came through the surgery. The doctors and nurses were pleased with the results. *20/20* asked to be there to film us when we first saw him, but Russel and I wanted to be alone with him. In the recovery room, Nathaniel was still asleep. He wasn't super swollen yet—that would come later. He had a cage mounted on his face and skull, just like the one we'd seen on Izzy. It was hard to look at, but his face was still our same beautiful Nathaniel. I hadn't expected him to look so peaceful.

We came out of the room and told the *20/20* cameras what we'd seen and how we felt. After we said good-bye to the crew, we were still standing right outside the door to the pediatric intensive care unit (PICU) when the doctors emerged. One of the key surgeons on Dr. Hopper's team was Dr. Kaalan Johnson. The same Dr. Johnson who had worked so hard to open his airway in Cincinnati! We felt lucky that he was in expert and familiar hands.

When the doctors came out, it had been four hours since they finished the surgery. Nathaniel was still asleep, and they'd just checked on him for the last time. Now they were heading home to get some much-needed rest.

After they told us that everything still looked good, they said, "Go to the hotel. You need rest too. He's going to sleep for a long time. He won't remember any-thing about tonight."

"Oh no," I said. "I've never done that before. I'll stay with him."

I knew the doctors were right: after such a long sur-gery, Nathaniel would most likely sleep through the night. But what if he woke up? Even though this time his eyes were sewn shut, I wanted him to "see" me and Russel right away. Ever since I'd kept vigil in a chair next to his bassinet in the NICU, I never left his side during or after a surgery, not even to get food while he slept. I barely went to the bathroom. And that's exactly what I planned to do now: to sit next to him on the chair, indefinitely.

Russel said, "She's going to be hard to convince."

But the doctors said, "Trust us, it's going to be fine."

Russel and I went back in to say goodnight. Nathaniel was still resting comfortably.

So we went back to the hotel, had a bottle of wine, and watched a movie. We picked a bad movie for unwinding—it was about a man being attacked by a bear and trying to survive in the wilderness—nonetheless, we managed to fall asleep around midnight.

At four in the morning the phone rang, a startling interruption in the quiet night. A voice said, "We have an emergency. Please come to the PICU *as soon as possible*. Nathaniel is flatlining."

Flatlining meant that the electronic monitor showed that his heart had stopped. This is the worst fear that anyone has when a loved one goes into surgery. In all the surgeries Nathaniel had undergone, he had only come close to death once before.

NATHANIEL I don't remember the first time I almost died, and it's a story that I haven't heard as often as the other ones because my mom doesn't like telling it. But everything worked out okay, so it doesn't bother me.

ZAP! FLASHBACK!

MAGDA When Nathaniel was two years old, we went to see an ear, nose, and throat doctor (ENT) who was not his regular doctor. This doctor was very well-known and respected. After a few appointments he looked at Nathaniel's CT scan, the structure of his face, his muscles and bones, and said, "All my life I've done impossible things. I can fix his airway and remove the trach. Trust me, I can do this." He was utterly confident.

We called our doctors at NYU to ask what they thought about this new doctor and his proposal. They said that he was known to be a wonderful surgeon, and it was possible that he might have success where they had struggled. Dr. Bernstein had already tried to remove the trach three separate times, starting after Nathaniel's first jaw surgery. Every time he tried, he had gone into the operating room with Nathaniel and come right back out fifteen minutes later. He'd say, "The bone is thicker than I thought, and it's close to his brain. I can't do it."

Now Dr. Bernstein and our other doctors encouraged us to let the Charlotte doctor give it a try.

Just before the surgery, the doctor came out to the room where Russel and I were waiting. For some reason I remember that he was wearing a white turtleneck under his scrubs.

"Let's pray to Jesus Christ so he guides my hand in the right direction," he said, reaching for our hands. Russel and I looked at each other. I don't like to mix religion and science, and I had never encountered a doctor who did, but there was no harm in being operated on by a good Christian man.

Russel said, "Praying never hurt."

"From your mouth to God's ears," I said.

Three hours passed while the doctor worked on Nathaniel. This seemed promising. Dr. Bernstein had always come out of the OR so quickly with the disappointing news that he couldn't do anything. I was thinking, *Oh my God, it's happening! This doctor is going to be successful!*

Finally, the doctor emerged, white as a ghost. He sat us down in a private room and said, "I am very sorry, my hand slipped. I went too far. I poked your son's brain with the drill. I made a hole. His brain fluid is leaking through his nose."

"What?!" Russel was shocked. We both were.

The doctor explained that they had plugged the hole and put two feet of bandages into Nathaniel's nose.

"Is he going to be brain damaged?" I asked the doctor.

"I just don't know," the doctor said. "If bacteria got in the brain, anything is possible."

I did not take the news of this incident calmly. My first thought was, *I'm not going to get my son back.* I went into shock, pulling fists of hair from my head. Hair actually came out of my head. I don't know how I did it. I must have pulled really hard.

When toddler Nathaniel came out of the OR, he was still unconscious. I lay down on the bed next to him, holding his hand and crying as I imagined him waking up and not knowing who I was.

Finally, Nathaniel opened his eyes. He took one look at my face, stroked my back and said, "It's okay, Mommy." And it was.

MÁGDA I knew that Dr. Hopper and Dr. Johnson hadn't put the Big Surgery in God's hands. They had been studying Nathaniel's physiology for more than a year! But what happened that night nobody could have predicted.

The voice on the phone told me that Nathaniel had flatlined. I was half asleep, but when I hung up I thought my son was dead. For some reason I called my mother and told her so. I don't remember how Russel and I got to the hospital. All I know is that when I walked into the room I saw right away that the monitors were on and he was stable. Nathaniel had lost his heart rhythm for twenty-two awful seconds. Thanks to an amazing nurse and a few quick chest compressions, he had regained rhythm quickly. He was back. The doctors reassured us that there was no loss of oxygen and no broken ribs, so no long-term effects. They believed the incident was caused by a new sedation medication or an infection in his heart, but they couldn't be sure which it was.

Russel was thanking the nurses for saving Nathaniel's life, telling them how grateful we were for them. But I barely registered any of it. I was sitting on the floor, rocking back and forth, pulling my hair. It was the same surge of overwhelming shock that I experienced when the doctor in North Carolina told me he had poked Nathaniel's brain. (Sorry, I know it's not a pretty image.)

NATHANIEL One of the medicines they gave me when I was asleep stopped my heart. Of course I had no idea this had happened, but a few days later, when I had my sight back and was able to write on my little tablet, I told my parents that I had dreamed I was in a blank room, and that our dog Coco was there, jumping on my chest and telling me to wake up. I didn't want to wake up because I was happy to see her and wanted to play with her.

When I told my mom the dream about Coco pounding on my chest, she got a weird look on her face. That's when she first told me that I'd been clinically dead for twenty-two seconds and that the doctors had used chest compressions to bring me back to life. I had died and come back to life! Coco had helped! (Though the doctors and nurses also deserve some credit.)

We were all pretty blown away by that one. Coco had been gone for two years and was barely in my dreams anymore. But when I was dying, it felt like Coco had decided to help and comfort me.

Dark Days

NATHANIEL The first few days after the surgery were really bad, and I never say that about surgeries. But my eyes were sewn closed. I couldn't wear my hearing aid. There was nothing for me to do to distract myself. I couldn't even eat yummy food because my jaw was wired shut. I couldn't lie down with the halo on, so, asleep or awake, I was sitting up.

It was dark and quiet all the time, so the only way I knew it was daytime was when I felt awake and alert, but what difference did it make? I was trapped in the darkness, still drugged up, falling asleep and waking up. I hated that part. My parents took turns holding my hand so I always knew someone was there. When they went to bathroom or coffee, they said, "Squeeze my hand twice if that's okay." Three squeezes meant I love you. Four meant I love you too.

My parents made small talk, filling the time talking about anything they could think of. My favorite story took place when Smokey was still a puppy. We went to visit Uncle Hal and Aunt Nancy, who had moved from Long Island to a farm in Rhode Island. They grew vegetables and had roosters and chickens. As you might imagine, my mom felt very at home there.

We were staying in the guest house, which was connected to the main house by a bridge. There was an outside staircase leading up to it, and every morning at five the roosters would start crowing and curious chickens would come up the stairs to see who was staying in the guest house. Smokey would bark like crazy.

One morning my mom woke up to the sound of screaming. She ran downstairs and saw Aunt Nancy in pajamas, one flip-flop, her hair a mess, waving a long stick in her hand. My dad was yelling, "Smokey, NO!" And Smokey was standing in the bushes, holding Domino, the biggest, most beautiful rooster, by the tail, shaking him.

Finally, Smokey let go of Domino, who in that life-and-death moment figured out how to fly and flapped over the fence to the cow farm next door. Smokey had blood and some of Domino's black-and-white feathers in his mouth. We found Domino's huge tail nearby, and the poor rooster was crowing next door. He had survived, but among the roosters, he had lost his status. He instantly went from high-ranking to low-ranking.

Smokey had to be on the leash for the rest of that trip, and we never brought him back to my aunt and uncle's house.

I loved that story, except that it made me laugh and, in my state, I was completely incapable of laughing. But I signaled my mom to tell it again and again.

There were more complications to this surgery than I'd ever had before. I kept thinking I was about to feel better when another issue would come up. I'd get sick, or they'd decide I needed another procedure.

I've been in hospitals enough to know my way around. I don't worry. I just go with it. If spending so much of my life so far in the hospital gave me any superpower, it was the ability to ignore pain. Flying or turning invisible would have been better, it's true, but everyone knows that you don't get to choose your superpower. It chooses you.

My face—the main focus of everything we were doing—was coming along great. But my stupid eye, which was supposed to be a minor side surgery, just kept causing problems. Everything that could go wrong did.

MAGDA The doctors were working on the structure of Nathaniel's eye sockets. It actually had nothing to do with his vision, although his vision had never been great. It was our fault—his vision would have been better except for a choice his dad and I made when he was little.

NATHANIEL There was a lot of me to fix, so my parents didn't fix everything. Even though I can't remember what happened with my eye, I'm glad to know that they listened to my opinion.

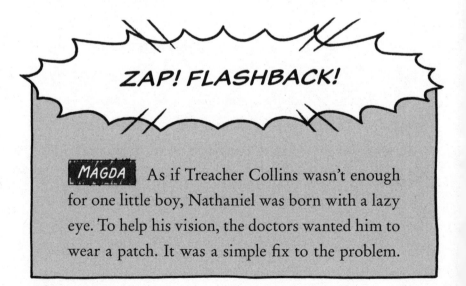

ZAP! FLASHBACK!

MAGDA As if Treacher Collins wasn't enough for one little boy, Nathaniel was born with a lazy eye. To help his vision, the doctors wanted him to wear a patch. It was a simple fix to the problem.

The patch went over his good eye, forcing the lazy eye to step up to the plate. It had to be done when he was young, or his brain would give up on the lesser eye.

This was right before kindergarten. Nathaniel was four years old, and he had a lot of facial surgeries coming up. For him, having only one good eye was a bit riskier than it is for an average person (like me—I also have a lazy eye that I've ignored my whole life). If during a surgery something went wrong with the good eye, he'd be left with a lazy eye that barely functioned.

The problem was, when we put the patch on him, he was so blind that he crashed into walls. He couldn't tell the difference between his blue Thomas train and his red James train. He was legally blind. It was a disaster. If Nathaniel recognized the hearing aid as a miracle, then the patch was a curse. He hated it, cried the whole time it was on, and tried to take it off. When he went in for surgery, having the patch on meant he couldn't even play or watch videos to distract himself from the pain.

Finally, we gave up. Nathaniel's life had so many complex, traumatic elements—the g-tube, the trach, the jaw surgeries—but this minor-seeming thing, a pirate patch that another kid might wear for fun, seemed to be the one thing that would torture him. I thought about what Dr. McCarthy had told us: "We can fix a broken bone if he falls on the playground, but if you don't let him have a normal childhood, we won't be able to fix his psyche."

In the scheme of priorities for Nathaniel, we decided better eyesight wasn't worth it. His sanity was more important. Nowadays, he doesn't remember how much he hated that patch, so maybe we should have made him wear it. Or maybe that trauma would have pushed him over the edge. We'll never know if we did the right thing.

MÁGDA Now we had taken away his vision and his hearing (mostly) and were definitely putting his sanity to the test, and although he was unhappy, he never got scared. He never panicked. He handled it with incredible grace. Like my dad, he has a remarkable ability to shift his focus from physical pain to other things.

After two days, his eyes were open, but he couldn't talk. The only way he could communicate was to write, but even that was hard. The first words he wrote in shaky, large letters on the LCD tablet we handed him were "no more drugs." He hated the jumbled feeling of the painkillers more than he minded the pain.

Watching him endure this, we questioned our choices each and every day. Life with a trach hadn't been so bad, had it? Why were we putting him through this? Were we the worst parents on the planet? Was this just too much?

NATHANIEL I didn't think about questioning our decision. I had already made the choice. It had been within my power and now I was living it out. I guess I've been going through surgeries and recoveries for such a long time that it's not a big emotional thing for me.

The only thing that made me mad was when my mom and Izzy's mom played scientists, discussing my recovery in detail. Izzy came to the hospital for some follow-up appointments. She was a few months ahead of me, but I had more complications, so my mom would say, "Look at him. Did this happen to Izzy?" My lazy eye got so much "lazier" that you couldn't see the pupil anymore. The two moms leaned right in my face, staring at my eye, and they came to the random, unscientific conclusion that video games had caused my lazy eye. It made no sense to me, and I did not appreciate the idea that they might take away the one survival tool at my disposal.

That eye was so annoying—at some point I just wanted them to give up on it. They ended up doing seven procedures after the big surgery, and when I say "procedures," I mean I had to be put to sleep while they fixed something. Anyone else would call that a "surgery."

I wanted to go home. I wanted to see my puppies. I don't like being hooked up to things, and there were a million devices attached to me, beeping and whirring, measuring my heart rate, my oxygen level.

Frustrations

NATHANIEL Six days after the surgery, I went to the Ronald McDonald House to recover. The Ronald McDonald House is a charity that gives families places to stay in times of need. We stayed in a hotel-like room, and there was a communal kitchen on the first floor.

I was still so swollen that I couldn't see well. Little by little, I could open one eye and try to watch a movie or play a video game.

With my jaw wired shut, I couldn't speak for a long time following the surgery. I'd want help walking to the bathroom, and my mother would sit there pointing from toy to toy. Or after I ate (through the g-tube) I wouldn't be full. My writing pad wasn't always handy, or I was supposed to keep my neck still. I growled. I hissed. I can't say I felt entirely patient.

Just when I was in this less-than-cheerful state, Jacob came to visit. He had been in Reno with my dad, attending lacrosse camp. Little brothers are annoying, but every little brother is annoying in his own way. Jacob knows me. He knows what I don't like, and he is very good at making it look to everyone else like he is trying to be nice. I don't like it when he offers me food. I don't like it when he reminds me to do stuff. I don't like it when he comes into my room and touches my stuff. When I get mad, my reaction seems mean when he knows perfectly well that he is provoking me.

Jacob is like my dad. He shows his emotions more. He screams when he's upset and cries when he's sad. Mom and I feel it but don't show it. I know he's a good person, but we're so different. Different interests. Different friends. We fight the way brothers do.

Jacob worries about me. He wants to take care of me. This is a loving way to be, but I don't like it. He treats me like a damsel in distress. It's nice that he wants to protect me, but I don't want him to feel like he has to. It makes me mad to have anyone look at me as weak. Especially my younger brother. If anything, I should be the one protecting him.

When Jacob talks about visiting me at the Ronald McDonald House, he says he was really excited to see me, and he wanted to talk and play, but as soon as he walked into the room he realized that I wouldn't be able to do anything but play video games. So he was kind of disappointed, but let's just remember who had more reason to be glum at that moment.

MÁGDA   When he first arrived, Jacob kept Nathaniel company while Russel and I went downstairs to prepare his food. Later, Jacob told us that as soon as we were gone, Nathaniel started crying. Jacob assumed it was because of the pain, but Nathaniel insists it was frustration. The way the halo was designed, a vertical metal bar was positioned right between his eyes. Imagine trying to focus while wearing a partial catcher's mask! He got headaches when he tried to play video games. To turn his head, he had to rotate his whole body. It was hard to sleep. Nathaniel couldn't talk, but he wrote a note to Jacob on his little pad, "Stop looking at me. I don't want you to see me like this."

A few days into his visit, Jacob was taking pride in helping his brother communicate. Nathaniel's mouth was wired shut, and Jacob was the best at understanding his speech. If Nathaniel said, "Hmm hmm hmm

hmm hmmm hmm" I couldn't figure it out and would ask him to repeat it, but Jacob knew he was saying, "I need to go to the bathroom."

NATHANIEL Two years before the big surgery, when we were making regular trips to Seattle so the doctors could figure out every detail of the operation, my dad and I went out to dinner near the hospital. A woman came up to us and said, "Hey, I just read a book called *Wonder* . . ." She and my dad started talking. I didn't pay close attention, but that conversation ended with me and my dad agreeing that I would visit her son's third grade class the next day, between appointments. Now she'd brought her son over, and I could hear him and Jacob were running around having fun in the Ronald McDonald House.

When I felt my worst, it was hard to look forward to getting rid of the trach. I was still just dreaming of eating pasta and swimming underwater. So I was sitting in bed in this near-constant state of frustration when I heard Jacob in the hallway plotting with his friend. Then he ran into my room, hit the wall above my head, and ran out. Then he did it again. I was a cannon, ready to explode. When Jacob hit the wall, it was like the Fourth of July. With my mouth wired shut

I couldn't yell at him to stop. I made a frustrated noise and stormed downstairs and ferociously typed on my iPad to tell my dad. I know he was behaving like a normal little brother, but he was teasing me at my lowest point! He still thinks how mad I got is hysterically funny. I think he's half-jealous of the attention I get. You'd think he'd be over that. I keep trying to explain that I can do without the attention.

The best thing about the Ronald McDonald House was that they had service dogs to comfort the kids who were recovering there. All the dogs were calm and collected, the way normal service dogs are supposed to be. But there was one—I can't remember his name, but he was an Australian shepherd—that acted completely unlike a service dog with me. When he saw me in my cage, he did not sit quietly. He came over to me and acted worried. He tried to lick me through the cage. He wanted to take care of me. That shepherd became my special buddy. She wouldn't leave my side. The other dogs sat quietly, waiting to be petted, but that dog wanted to be in my lap cuddling. It was the next best thing to reuniting with my own dogs.

We've Got This

NATHANIEL I'd had several jaw surgeries, and every time I had one, there were screws that needed to be tightened daily in order to slowly expand my bones. While I was in the Ronald McDonald House my parents did the same thing, there were just more screws than ever before. At first when they twisted the screws, I didn't feel it. But just as it gets harder to tighten anything you're twisting into place, it got more unpleasant the more they turned. It was an aching pain. After three weeks, when they thought they'd gone as far as possible, when I'd been stretched as far as a kid could likely be stretched, and the X rays confirmed it, we locked everything in place. The halo would stay on and my jaws, which would be wired shut until the bone healed—four months total.

MAGDA The expansion had taken less time than the doctors had anticipated, and the doctor said, "Everything is good. He's stable and you know what you're doing. You can go home for two or three weeks until your next checkup."

We had our room at the Ronald McDonald House for a few more weeks, but Nathaniel would thrive best at home in Reno, in his own environment, with the dogs to comfort him.

We knew how to take care of him, even if it still didn't come easily to me. I remembered the first time I had tried to suction Nathaniel's trach—he gagged and I promptly threw up. I'd come a long way since then, but I would never be a natural nurse. Whenever Russel was around, Nathaniel would ask him to handle medical procedures instead of me. He'd say, "I love her, Dad, but you've got to do it. She's not gentle."

Russel and Jacob were already back home. The day after the doctor set us free, I packed up the whole room, cleaned, and put everything in the car. Nathaniel and I set out at seven the next morning on the twelve-hour drive to Reno. Nathaniel was semireclined in the passenger seat, surrounded by pillows. Every three hours I stopped and fed him. I sanitized my hands and the syringe using antibacterial wipes and a bottle of water. It wasn't exactly a sterile environment, and it got worse. I took a "shortcut," avoiding the main roads, because when we pulled over to feed him, I wanted privacy. The down side to this was that our route had very curvy roads.

We were making good progress when suddenly Nathaniel tapped my arm and gestured wildly. I looked over and saw a panicked look in his eyes. His face was turning purple. He was throwing up—except that he couldn't throw up because his jaw was still wired shut! He was choking! I reached over and opened the trach (which would stay in place until he healed), and vomit came out through the hole. After I pulled over, I suctioned the trach. Then I thought about how much trouble we'd be in if there was a real emergency. There had been no gas station and no cell signal for miles, and there was no sign of anything ahead. There were no other cars on the road. We were in the middle of nowhere, with no help if we needed it. I got us headed back toward civilization as quickly as possible.

Outside of Reno the roads were very dark. We were driving through the desert on a divided highway when I noticed a car right next to me, going very slowly with its hazard lights blinking. It was strange. I thought maybe it was a carjacker or some weirdo, so I kept my eyes focused straight ahead. A moment later, I almost hit a horse. A horse! I pulled over on the shoulder and saw that there were many horses running in the parkway. Cars had their hazards on to alert other drivers as Animal Control tried to herd the horses out of the road. Of all the obstacles I anticipated when driving my caged son home, wild horses on the median had not made the list.

NATHANIEL For the record, normally I could have been a quick thinker and opened my trach myself, but I was panicking because I hadn't anticipated that it might happen. I really thought I might suffocate. As soon as she opened the trach, I was relieved to be able to breathe. We pulled over and cleaned up as best we could. It was bad in the moment but I didn't dwell on it.

Because my mouth was wired shut, I was back to "eating" liquids through a g-tube for the first time since I was a little kid.

My mom has always told me about how when I was a baby, formula made me barf, so it was funny/not funny to discover that now, having a g-tube again at twelve, I found her story to be true. At first, in the Ronald McDonald House, they tried feeding me formula and I felt nauseated all the time. It got better as soon as I was allowed regular food (that had been liquefied). While I was being fed, I played on my iPad.

Being fed through a tube wasn't satisfying. It's a strange sensation, to "eat" and get full without ever tasting a bite. When I was done I still wanted food in my mouth. It was like watching a movie without being able to hear anything. I could feel the temperature of the food. If it was really hot, I'd feel the warmth in my belly, but it was summer, so I preferred cold foods. Above all, I was really dying for pasta. Mom made it for me, but of course I couldn't taste it. Spaghetti and meatballs through a tube directly to your stomach just isn't the same. At first my parents wanted us to have meals together as a family, but I didn't like watching them eat. It felt like I was being teased.

Mom taught Jacob how to feed me—for "emergencies" she said, but I'd rather have eaten a porcupine than let my brother feed me. I wasn't allowing him near a hole in my stomach for multiple reasons. He's good at lacrosse, but I was not confident in his g-tube technique.

When I felt my worst, it was hard to believe this surgery was a good idea. It was hard to look forward to getting rid of the trach. I was still just dreaming of eating pasta and swimming underwater.

PART V

DOUBLE
TROUBLE

Lightning Strikes Twice

NATHANIEL Gradually, I started feeling better. Our three dogs helped. When Mom and I got home from the Ronald McDonald House, Dad had them locked in a room away from the door so that they wouldn't jump on me. I went and sat on the couch, then he let them out. Amazingly, they knew to be gentle. I hugged whoever came within my reach. Snowball looked up at me, sniffing, checking on me. Brownie was the most confused. He stood at a distance staring at me. I probably smelled like blood and puke.

I had been home in Reno for four weeks. Dad had a new job in Connecticut. At first, right after the surgery, he just went to meetings occasionally, but now that I was feeling better, he made plans to go there for the week and come home on weekends. When I was all better the plan was to move back to the East Coast,

231

but I still had a cage on my head, two more months before it came off. After that the doctors thought I would need about six months of healing before they could try to remove the trach.

School was still in session, and everyone started asking to come visit me. Instead, my mom arranged for me to go to school, show them that I was okay, and say good-bye because I'd be at school in Connecticut for seventh grade.

As I was hanging out with my classmates, nodding my heavy halo to answer their questions, I heard my dad and the teacher talking. It sounded like she was trying to sneak in some homework for me. There was no way I was going to let that happen. My attention span was short, and I was having trouble focusing on anything. I didn't think I could handle work, and I definitely didn't want to try. I got Dad away from that teacher as fast as I could.

Then something unexpectedly awful happened.

MAGDA I just had a cough. I figured it was allergies, so I stopped by the doctor to get it checked out. He took an X ray, told me he saw a tumor in my lungs that didn't look good, and sent me to an oncologist, a doctor who is a cancer specialist. Ridiculous! I couldn't possibly have cancer. I was sure of this because, believe it or not, I had already had cancer once! That time, I had felt very sick, like I was dying. I *was* dying. But all I had now was a cough. I was sure the doctor was wrong.

The next day, Nathaniel and I picked up Jacob from lacrosse practice. (I wasn't comfortable leaving Nathaniel alone, so when I had to go out, I always brought him with me, cage and all.) The doctor called with the results of a test. I was so sure that there was nothing to worry about that I had the doctor on speaker in the car when he told me I really did have cancer. Again.

Yeah, if I'd known I was going to get bad news, I definitely would not have had the doctor on speaker. I would have preferred to break the news to the kids gently, after absorbing it myself, but now, in the back seat, both kids immediately started crying.

"Are you going to die?" they wanted to know.

"They still don't know what they're talking about," I told them. But a dark shadow of dread had already started to come over me.

The First Lightning Strike

NATHANIEL I don't remember when my mother had cancer for the first time because I was only two years old, but the story came up a lot when she got diagnosed for the second time. It reminded us all how strong she was.

ZAP! FLASHBACK!

MAGDA Jacob was a newborn. My pregnancy had gone smoothly. All through it, I was mowing the lawn, cleaning the house, playing with Nathaniel, eating good food, and getting plenty of sleep. I looked healthy. But after that horrible surgery when the doctor accidentally poked

Nathaniel's brain (Nathaniel laughs every time I describe it that way), my energy changed. For the next month, I constantly hovered near Nathaniel to see if there was leakage. I was always nervous, always on edge.

Within a week of giving birth to Jacob I lost way too much weight too quickly. The glands behind my ears swelled up. They looked like eggs. I went to the family doctor, who told me it was nothing to worry about. They thought I had anemia, an iron deficiency. They told me to increase the iron in my diet.

A week or two later I felt like I was having a panic attack. I couldn't breathe. I went to the emergency room where they did an electrocardiogram (an EKG) to check the electrical activity of my heart and make sure I wasn't having a heart attack. Next, I had an awful pain in the middle of my spine.

My mother came to visit and found me weighing ninety pounds. (Have I mentioned that I'm five feet seven?) She said, "Your skin is the color of dirt. What is wrong with you? Something's wrong."

Nobody paid attention to my swollen glands. Various doctors thought it was stress, a cold or flu, or maybe postpartum depression, which is a temporary mood change that can come after a pregnancy. I believed the doctors, but I was feeling worse and worse. By the time Jacob was four months old, I couldn't get warm. My whole jaw ached from my teeth chattering.

My father came to visit. At one point he was downstairs, and I was up in our bedroom, shaking so much that I was having weird little spasms. It was hard to utter a word through my chattering teeth. I managed to moan, "Dad," loudly enough for him to hear me.

He came up to my room and asked, "What's the matter?"

I had three blankets piled on the bed and asked him for a fourth.

"Magda, something is seriously wrong with you. I think you're really sick," he said. "What kind of doctor did you go to?" and then he went down the road that any parent of an immigrant has traveled: "Why did you come to this country? Look what is happening to you. You should come back to Poland with me."

A week after my dad left, I could no longer walk up the stairs. I'd crawl up on all fours and slide back down on my butt, sometimes with the baby snug under one arm. I sat on the floor to prepare meals, peeling potatoes as I leaned against the cabinet, bowl between my legs, like a rag doll Cinderella. To an outsider it probably looked like I was practicing a new parenting philosophy: Be on their level! Show them how to crawl! It's not a hard rule to follow if standing up to change a diaper puts you in excruciating pain.

Russel was at the end of his rope. He worked all day and came home to a household that was holding on by a thread. The strain began to show. One night I was up in my room shivering and I overheard him on the phone downstairs.

"Magda is really faking it. She says she can't breathe, she can't walk, she's in pain. All the doctors say it's in her head. I've been dealing with this for four months."

I thought, *I'm dying. I'm literally dying.* I crawled down the hall to the top of the stairs and spoke to Russel through the spindles of the banister, "Look at me. I'm not making this up. I've never had pain like this. My body is failing me. I'm dying! If you don't take me to a doctor tomorrow morning I'm going back to Poland where my family who loves me will save my life."

I went to sleep. Russel made an appointment with a doctor for the next morning, but he wasn't happy about it. He shook me awake at seven saying, "Get out of bed" in a mean voice, like I was a lazy bum. I drove myself to the doctor. On the way there I threw up green, all over myself and all over the car, like I had been eating spinach. (Nathaniel wasn't the only one in our family to throw up in a car.)

The doctor greeted me, "Hi, Mrs. Newman, what brings you in?" He had a cheerful voice. He felt my nodes. I could barely talk. Suddenly his face was serious. "I see that you're underweight. Let's X-ray your lungs."

They brought an X ray machine into the room. Ten minutes later the doctor came back with paperwork. He said, "Well, Mrs. Newman, first we have to do some blood work, but even without looking at that I feel sure that you have cancer."

Crying hysterically, I grabbed his shoulders and said, "Thank you." I know it sounds funny that hearing I had cancer was good news, but it meant I wasn't crazy.

I called Russel to tell him they were doing bloodwork to confirm cancer. He came straight to the doctor's office, got down on his knees in front of me and the doctor and begged me to forgive him. "I failed you. I never deserved you in the first place, and I failed you."

I didn't dwell on Russel's mistake. I understood it. I had gone to so many doctors, and it looked to everyone like I was faking. They were all so convincing that I myself had started to believe them.

I had a four-month old baby, a two-year-old with Treacher Collins, and a blood cancer called Hodgkin's lymphoma that had spread all over my body.

The cancer treatment was chemotherapy. From the outside, it just looks like a tube of medicine going into your body. I had to go to the doctor's office to receive the medicine for several hours at a time, every two weeks for twelve rounds. The chemo makes you better, but it makes you feel worse. After an hour or so I would get a weird metallic taste in my mouth. Eventually I lost my sense of taste and smell and felt nauseated all the time. But when the doctors did scans to see the cancer in my body, the tumors were shrinking. My back didn't hurt anymore. I knew it would be worth it.

One night, after the chemo had started to take its toll on me, Russel saw Nathaniel walk into our room where I was sleeping. He had just become a big brother and, ever since then, his mother hadn't been the same. As Russel watched, he stuck out his little hand and appeared to sprinkle something on my head.

"What are you doing to Mommy?" Russel asked.

"I'm sprinkling magic dust on her so she gets better," Nathaniel said.

Russel cried when Nathaniel said this, and he cried when he told it to me, and he cries every time he tells that story. He says, "However flawed I was, I was raising a little boy who, for all his own challenges, was determined to help and heal his mother."

NATHANIEL When Mom was diagnosed with cancer for the second time, she found a doctor in a special cancer center that happened to be in . . . Seattle! Now that half of our family was seeing doctors in Seattle, we decided to move there full-time. One day we were moving to Connecticut for my dad's job, the next day we were moving to Seattle for my mom's cancer. If it hadn't been impossible to move my neck, I might have gotten whiplash. We left Reno so quickly that I didn't get to say good-bye to some of my best friends. Now, half of our family was sick. If Mom was upset, she didn't show it, and I don't react much on the outside either, but on the inside I worried a lot. To make it better, I said to myself, *She's going to be fine. My mom is really strong.* I felt believing something will happen helps it come true.

MAGDA Uprooting ten-year-old Jacob for the fifth time in his life, and twelve-year-old Nathaniel for the seventh, we bought a second car, stuffed everything we could fit into the two cars, including the three dogs and Nathaniel with a cage around his head needing to be fed every three hours through a tube, and moved ourselves to Seattle in time for my Monday morning doctor's appointment.

We put the house in Reno up for sale. I left it spotless, walking out backwards so there were no footprints.

Disguises

MAGDA One of the side effects of chemo is that it makes your hair fall out. It doesn't hurt, but it's rather surprising to adopt a dramatic new hairdo—bald!— whether you like it or not. The first time I got cancer I prepared for the inevitable hair loss by going to a wig-maker in Charlotte. She studied my face and my coloring and then created a $250 custom wig for me from real hair. I did not love it. This time I ordered a few fun wigs on Amazon: a purple one, a short one, and one with long blonde hair coming out from under a baseball cap. And that's how I went into cancer number two. Like a purple-haired warrior.

I went to a hairdresser the day before my first round of chemo. I didn't tell her I had cancer. I just said, "I want to shave my head!"

She was so excited. She said, "Have you ever done it before?"

I said, "No."

I chose to embrace life, to fight for myself and for the best life I could give my boys. I refused to believe I would die. I was as strong as I'd ever been in my life, and I was ready to win. I told myself that I would be okay, that I had the kids to live for. My underlying belief was that God exists. Because thinking positive is one way of having faith.

With my fun wigs, I wanted to avoid people looking at me with pity.

Nathaniel was noticed by strangers from the moment he was born, and from that day on, without asking for attention, without saying a word. He wasn't given the choice. I, as his mother, received similar attention. The unspoken questions were: "What's wrong with you to have a child like that? What's wrong with your child?" When I was a competitive pianist, I liked being on stage. Having an audience energized me. But this was different. After years of Nathaniel getting stares for his disability, I had no desire to draw that kind of attention to myself.

Beauty is an accident just as much as Treacher Collins is an accident, but your appearance in any extreme shapes you. When I was young, I enjoyed being looked at, being a young girl and feeling pretty. Seeing people respond to Nathaniel changed my relationship with beauty. People care so much about appearance, and here I was with a child who would never fit into the normal idea of beauty. I stopped seeing beauty as an external quality. It's easy to say that beauty is within—that's not a new message—but it became very real for me. I found true beauty in the people who reacted to my child with care, love, hope, joy.

NATHANIEL I don't overthink my appearance. When I look at baby pictures of myself, I just see a baby. Sure, there are some tubes and contraptions, but all babies seem to have a lot of gear. My experience looks like one thing on the outside, but I was just a kid, born the way I was. As I got older, the face that I saw in the mirror made sense to me. Visits to doctors were routine. I grew up with the understanding that my face was more complicated than everyone else's—it didn't work as well—but that was my world.

Some kid might have to deal with his or her helicopter mom, twin brother, or asthma. I think you have to lose something to feel the loss. I was born this way, and my parents loved me just the same. They always told me that being different made me interesting. Maybe that's why it didn't occur to me to feel sorry for myself, or even to focus on the mirror. I have always just felt like myself. I don't even notice my scars unless I'm focusing on them. I see what I want to see.

When it comes to Treacher Collins, I find the positive. I can turn off my hearing aid when my brother is being annoying, and because my BAHA has Bluetooth, I can listen to music or watch movies on the plane without headphones. That's right—I can play music in my head. Pretty bionic. And for some reason, one feature of Treacher Collins is that I have extra hair on my body, including my face. My mom asked if I wanted to shave the sideburns on my cheeks, but I like them. I'm not trying to look like everyone else. I'd rather look like Wolverine. Also, considering I have a fairly severe case of Treacher Collins, I'd say I'm pretty hot.

Uncaged

NATHANIEL Four months after the Big Surgery, on August 9, it was time for the halo to come off. Even better, they were going to unwire my jaws. I was so excited to eat. They warned me that I wouldn't be able to eat solid foods right away, but I had a whole plan: spaghetti and meatballs as soon as possible. Then pudding and Baskin-Robbins. Mushed-up baked beans and mac 'n' cheese next. And a Hebrew National hot dog soon thereafter.

This was another eleven-hour surgery that started at 8:15 a.m. My mom's cancer treatments were making her really sick, and her doctors didn't want her anywhere near the hospital, but she came anyway, of course. I sat on her lap all morning, until Dad carried me into the operating room.

Removing the halo was the easy part of the surgery. The doctors also worked on reconstructing Nathaniel's cheekbones and eye sockets. This was very important—it would mean that Nathaniel's eyes were protected and sat in the right place relative to his new facial structure. It would also change his appearance, which made us a tiny bit sad. His perfectly imperfect face needed no changing, but this was about the safety of his precious eyes.

It was hard not to be waiting in the hospital with Russel the way I usually did. To go back home, lying sick in bed, felt like a failure. I wanted to be there to protect my son.

After getting texts about the surgery's progress throughout the day, I came back to the hospital and was waiting in the recovery room when they brought out Nathaniel. To see Nathaniel's new face floored us. It was as if Dr. Hopper and his team had given Nathaniel the face he was intended to have.

Russel and I kept looking at Nathaniel, then at each other, then at Nathaniel, and back at each other. Just filled with emotions. Did we miss the old face? Would he?

I insist that Nathaniel was named after a mythical Scandinavian prince from my childhood books, but

Russel likes to say that he was named after Russel's grandfather Norman Koslow. In that moment, Russel saw his *popi* in Nathaniel's face. He turned to me and said, "Nathaniel is a Koslow through and through. A surgeon has restored my son to what God or nature intended all along."

The day was a great success. A parent's job is to raise his children to go out into the world independently. Every step closer we got to removing the trach felt like Nathaniel was catching up to the level of independence that other kids his age came to naturally. He had paid a high price, but if the trach came out, it would all be worth it. We were very optimistic.

NATHANIEL I was not in the best shape when I woke up. I thought getting the halo off would feel good, like pressure had been relieved, but in fact it felt like a knife had been ripped out of my head. My eyes were swollen shut again. Being blind for two days is not an easy thing. It was scary. I thought I was going crazy, hearing voices. I don't think I was even on pain medicine. I always ask not to have it because it makes me feel gross. I prefer to ignore the pain. This sounds heroic, but it's actually easier to do when you've had surgery: a planned, calculated injury. If you stub your toe, it's a completely different kind of pain. It's out of nowhere. The element of surprise makes it harder to handle. But when pain slowly emerges, or comes about in a hospital, I am pretty good at pushing it away.

In spite of the pain, my head did feel much lighter without the halo—almost like I had super strength—and I felt like I'd come a long way.

Best of all, my jaws were free! The first meal I had was a big bowl of pasta and meatballs. It tasted soooo good. I'd been dreaming of this moment for so long. The doctors were right—I couldn't really chew, and I even had trouble swallowing. I think my muscles were really weak. But just being able to put food in my mouth—to taste real flavors—that in itself was a huge improvement. For the first time in my life I was happy just to know that I would be able to taste food every day. It felt like the best present I'd ever been given.

PART VI

Two Boy Wonders

Wonder Comes to Life

NATHANIEL   Only nine days after the cage came off, my family had a surprise for me. The *Wonder* movie was being filmed, and they had called, inviting us to visit the set. I wasn't exactly feeling one-hundred percent yet. Not even close! But I was excited to meet the actor playing Auggie, and I wanted to see how they were going to make him look like he had Treacher Collins.

They were shooting in Vancouver, British Columbia, a two-and-a-half-hour drive from Seattle. We exited a highway and drove to a trailer park near a big warehouse. There were no signs or indications that a movie was being shot, but there was security everywhere. On the doors of the trailers, in tiny letters, were the names of the actors, and we were led to a trailer they had set up just for me! All of R.J.'s books were there, editions she had signed saying, "We are all wonders."

Todd, the producer we knew best, brought us to the warehouse—which turned out to be the sound-stage where they were shooting the movie. To get in, we went through a tiny door with a person guarding it. If a red light was on, that meant they were filming, and nobody could go in or out until that light went off. Inside, there were wires everywhere. It made you wonder how none of the wires appeared in the shot. They told us to be quiet when they were filming and gave us headsets so we could hear what the actors were saying into their microphones.

When they called "cut," suddenly everyone started talking again, and running around to adjust things, and then suddenly they'd yell, "Rolling!" and we had to be as silent as mice.

Todd guided us through the movie sets for some of the rooms that would appear in the movie. There was a classroom, the kitchen in the Pullmans' house, Auggie's room. I was amazed at how real everything looked. On the bookshelves in Auggie's room there was Disney-related memorabilia. A gold Buzz Light-year from *Toy Story*. Something else from *Bambi*. My mom asked Todd if this was intentional, and he told us that Disney was producing the movie, so they put those items there as a funny little thank-you.

MÁGDA We watched the same scene being shot over and over again. I was fascinated to see how much work and time it took to get that one scene, especially because every time the actors did it, I thought, *That was perfect! Leave it!* And then they'd say, "Take number forty," and try again.

Todd asked for our "notes," and we gave him some feedback, although there was nothing significantly wrong. They had Auggie talking on the phone, and we told them that even with the hearing aid, talking on the phone doesn't really work for Nathaniel. We thought Auggie's eyes would be more realistic if they were a little droopier.

Jacob Tremblay was doing a great job, and I told him that I liked how he kept his head stiff. He said that he was worried about that stiffness. The prosthetic face was uncomfortable and restricted his movement. But with his trach and hearing aid—so many attachments— Nathaniel always walked carefully. So what Jacob was doing was authentic. Both heads were fragile.

Todd introduced us to the rest of the cast. I was pleasantly surprised by Owen Wilson, the well-known movie star who played Auggie's father. He made jokes with the kids, high-fiving them. A real what-you-see-is-what-you-get guy. When Jacob (Nathaniel's brother, not the actor Jacob Tremblay) said, "You sound like Lightning McQueen!" he said, "I *am* Lightning McQueen, and he made a *ka-chow* sound that we all recognized from *Cars*. He told us that *Cars 3* was coming out soon. It was cool for us to hear that news from one of the stars of the movie.

Julia Roberts, also a famous movie star, was kind and thoughtful. She brought Jacob and Nathaniel board games and gifts, and I noticed that she spent every break with her children, so I could tell she was a loving mom.

Jacob talked to Izabela Vidovic—who plays Auggie's sister, Via—about what it's like to have a sibling like Nathaniel. He suggested that she emphasize the part when she is slightly jealous of how Auggie gets more attention, but then devastated when her brother is hurt by a bully. I heard him telling her, "You gotta show how intense that is."

NATHANIEL My face was familiar to Jacob from the day he was born. He was the one person who had no idea that I was different until he saw people picking on me. He remembers that when he first heard people saying mean things, he looked at my face and couldn't see the difference. He'd been around people with craniofacial differences his whole life. Jacob grew up blind to "normal." But if you tell me I should feel grateful to have a little brother who always saw me for who I am, I will tell you that he's still a little brother, not an angel.

MAGDA I was wearing one of my wigs—blonde hair coming out from under a baseball cap. When we saw R.J., she came up and asked me how I was feeling. Someone asked what was going on. I said that I was battling cancer. There were young kids around, some of the siblings of the actors. One of them said, "If you had cancer, you'd be bald!"

I said, "It's a wig," but they didn't believe me. So I said, "You want to see?" and I pulled it off.

The kids thought it was wild, although it didn't seem quite so out of the ordinary on a movie set where a boy was wearing a custom mask that was handmade every day.

NATHANIEL Next, Todd led us to the make-up trailer. The makeup guy showed us how he made the prosthetic for Jacob's face. There were photos of me hanging on the wall for inspiration. I could not believe how much work it took to make a normal-looking kid look sort of like me, but not even as different.

MÁGDA Turning Jacob's face into Auggie's wasn't just a matter of some well-done makeup. There was a whole fake head, from a wig down to the top of his chest. The wig was attached to a mold of the face, and the prosthetic was basically goop that was piled up an inch thick and glued onto the mold of Jacob's face. A new one had to be made every day. There was a mechanism hidden under the gooey material that ran all the way from one eye down to his hand, where there was a button he could press to make his eye droop whenever the camera was on. Jacob said it was really hot in the mask.

I couldn't help thinking of the irony: it must have cost them a lot of money just to make the prosthetic face that Jacob wore to be Auggie. If they had hired someone whose face was naturally like that, they could have used all that money to change the lives of kids who needed help. But I reminded myself that spreading the story of kids with facial difference was the most important goal. The producers knew how to make the best movie, not me. And the better the movie, the farther the message would reach. That was worth much more than the cost of one prosthetic mask.

Besides, Jacob Tremblay was a perfect Auggie, even wearing that uncomfortable mask.

NATHANIEL When I first talked to Jacob Tremblay, he had the Auggie Pullman mask on. It was strange talking to a kid who didn't have Treacher Collins and looked exactly like he did, but the way someone looks isn't a big deal to me, so I almost forgot it was a mask. Until they took it off. Then it looked like they were pulling his actual face off. Creepy, yeah, but boy would it have been more convenient to peel off my face and call it a day than to endure the most recent four months of surgeries, and screws, and being in a cage.

We were on set for about eight hours. After seeing how slowly they moved forward, I don't know what anyone was thinking when they had me audition for Auggie! There's no way I could have spent day after day going slowly through the scenes. I would have lost my mind. It made me appreciate movies much more. The final movie is only two hours long. But making it takes months. What I learned from meeting

Jacob was that it's not as easy as people think. Those actors are endurance athletes.

Even though the halo was off, I felt weak all the time. My ribs were poking out. I'd barely eaten for four months so I was malnourished and my weight had dropped to fifty pounds. I got tired really easily, so after spending the day meeting actors, watching them shoot scenes, and exploring the set, we headed back to our hotel. The next day was Friday. We had breakfast with the whole cast. Then we hurried back to Seattle. My mom had to be in the hospital for chemo at two. We were so Hollywood.

MAGDA Our Thanksgiving tradition was to deepfry a turkey. In North Carolina, all of our neighbors had deep-fried their turkeys. I had my doubts, so one year, while I roasted one bird in the oven, Russel deepfried another in peanut oil. We had lots of guests that year, not all of them Southern, and when they left, the deep-fried turkey was picked clean. My roast turkey was basically untouched. We never looked back.

This was our first Thanksgiving in Seattle. It was raining, of course. Russel put up a tarp over part of the backyard to shelter the deep fryer while the rest of us—including my parents, who were visiting from

Poland—sat on the porch. Jacob made all the side dishes, and I was his sous-chef. It was still hard for Nathaniel to chew, but we cut up tiny pieces of turkey and mixed them in with Jacob's mashed potatoes. For some reason, Nathaniel never liked to eat Jacob's food. If Jacob made food for Nathaniel's g-tube, we hid that fact. He says he just didn't want to give his brother the satisfaction. But that Thanksgiving was the first time he didn't refuse to eat food that Jacob prepared.

Every year we like to go around the table saying what we are thankful for. This year it was a no-brainer. Every person at the table gave thanks, in one way or another, for all of our good health.

The day after Thanksgiving, Jacob and I drove one mile up the street to a corner where a guy was selling Christmas trees. The trees in Seattle were thick, full, storybook trees that smelled delicious. Our kids love to decorate the tree, but we call it a Hanumas tree, decorating it with blue ornaments, a little menorah ornament, and a sign saying HAPPY HANUKKAH. We have a video of Nathaniel standing in front of the tree, belting the Miley Cyrus song "Wrecking Ball" while his grandfather is in the background, cleaning the menorah. After all we'd been through, we were full of joy.

Made Whole Again

NATHANIEL   For ten months after the surgery I practiced breathing through my nose and sleeping with the trach capped. Even with the trach closed, my oxygen level never dropped below 97 percent, which meant I officially didn't need the trach anymore. If you looked at how I spent my waking hours during my whole life, "dealing with the trach" probably ranked first, although "being annoyed by Jacob" or "hugging my dogs" were both close in the running. I mean, if I'd spent as much time playing the piano as I had in hospitals trying to get rid of this trach, well, I probably could have been a concert pianist like my mother. But when it came to the trach, I wouldn't get a grade or receive a trophy for my efforts. I had to take everyone's word that my life without it would be changed for the better.

Finally, in late January, the time came to remove Nathaniel's trach. Nathaniel was able to sleep with the trach fully capped, his breath silent and sure. It was a miracle for this child who was born with a very complicated airway, a child who'd had sixty-plus surgeries and procedures. I was used to monitoring his breath, even in my sleep. And now, at night, he was so quiet as to make me nervous. When parents first bring a newborn baby home from the hospital, there's always a moment when they stare at the crib watching the baby's chest rise and fall peacefully. That night had eluded us for so long. Now it was ours.

"It's going to be so anticlimactic," Russel said the night before it was to come out. "Remove a few Velcro straps, slide out the trach, and slap a Band-Aid on it. Walk out of the hospital and be on our merry way. It's almost unfair! After thirteen years with a tracheostomy, thirteen years with a hole in his neck, thirteen years of "what's that in his throat—"

I chimed in, "Thirteen years of infections, thirteen years of suctioning, thirteen years of cleaning, thirteen years in a tub instead of a shower—"

And Nathaniel added, "Thirteen years of 'Don't go underwater like all the other kids,' thirteen years of nurses—"

We threw it all out there on the table: thirteen years of school challenges; thirteen years worried about a fall, a slip, a hit to the neck; thirteen years of checking oxygen levels; thirteen years of annoying calls with medical supply companies; thirteen years of meddling respiratory therapists; and, finally, thirteen years of questions about the future.

Russel said, "Thirteen years and I want marching bands! I want glitter falling from the sky!"

Then Nathaniel said, "Thirteen years of 'I'd like to know if I can bring my iPad and DS so I can watch movies and play games.'"

We all laughed.

Strangely, unexpectedly, Russel felt a little sad. He explained that we had spent precious moments with Nathaniel every night. Caring for him. Gently cleaning his trach. Was it straight? Was the Velcro tight enough or too tight? Should I use saline drops? When did we change it last? What's that smell? Is it infected? Suction? No suction?

Russel said to Nathaniel, "Promise me something. Promise I can always take care of you? Promise you will still need me?"

His response was classic Nathaniel, "Dad, I want my trach out. I never said I wanted them to take my

Treacher Collins away. I'll always need you and Momma."

Then he smiled and ran off to play Pokémon as if to say once again, *Stop making it a big deal, Dad. I got this.*

NATHANIEL A crowd gathered around my hospital bed. It was Mom, Dad, Jacob, Dr. Johnson, and the camera guy from *20/20*. It was kind of an intense moment, and it was also kind of a nothing moment. They took the trach out, something that we'd done every two weeks for my whole life, but this time, instead of putting a new one in, they bandaged the hole and threw the trach in the garbage. Just like that.

After they took it out, we sat for a few minutes and talked. It felt so weird, an absence. Breathing through my nose still wasn't instinctive. If I stopped paying attention, I went back to breathing through my mouth, and then it felt like my trach had come out and I couldn't get enough air without it. I was scared of losing my breath, and worried that without my trach I'd suffocate. I didn't like the feeling.

Suddenly, it occurred to me that maybe I would never get used to being without it. I'd had a trach my whole life. It was how I breathed. It had always been a part of my body; I never knew a time when it wasn't there. I couldn't grasp that I was going to live this way forever. Before, I had three ways of breathing—through my nose, my mouth, and my trach. Now I only had two, like everyone else. It felt like a loss. How could I feel comfortable eating and sleeping without an open trach?

I quietly asked my mom to send everyone out of the room. When they were gone, and it was just Mom and me, I said what was on my mind.

"I want my trach back. Can they put it back in?"

Mom said, "Let's just wait an hour and see what happens."

I knew, obviously, that this was the whole reason I'd had the surgery and that horrible heavy halo. This is what my parents and all the doctors wanted for me. They had all worked toward this, really hard, for a long time. It was supposed to be exciting, a huge success, and I was embarrassed to feel the way I did, but my trach was my security blanket. It always had a name. The name changed over time, but the most recent one I'd had was named Charlie Hudson. It was hard to let Charlie go.

MAGDA The trach just popped right out. This was why we'd had to be so careful with it—because it came out easily, and the minute it did, his body would start to heal itself. This was precisely what I had fought *against* for many years. What a strange feeling it was for the trach coming out to be the goal. The moment they removed it was . . . just a moment. They taped up the hole. Done. But that night, talking to Russel, I said, "All this suffering. All this came down to a single moment, that moment when the trach came out. We succeeded. It was all worth it."

Dr. Hopper hadn't waved a magic wand over Nathaniel. The surgery was still a new procedure and a learning process for the medical team. Nathaniel's body rejected some of the plates they put in his head and one of the implants in his face. The wound on his head didn't heal quickly. He needed to have twelve additional surgical procedures that Izzy, the child who went before him, hadn't needed. Sometimes we had hurried to the hospital five times in a week. He was on antibiotics for three months in case it had been an infection that stopped his heart. But here we were. Finally. It was a level of normal we had worked toward his whole life.

That night we had a huge steak dinner. Nathaniel loves a good rare steak. Russel said, "Ding-dong, the trach is gone."

NATHANIEL It would have been easier to be born "normal," but far less cool. At a craniofacial event a few years back, they had pictures of some kids with craniofacial conditions, and on each picture was the amount of money that their combined surgeries had cost. Mine were in the millions. I think it was $1.7 million. One of the highest. And that was before the halo. I'm proud of that. Not because of all the money that went toward me, but because it marks how much I've been through. I know how strong I am. I know I can tolerate pain. It's a weird sort of bragging rights.

I definitely don't miss the trach any more. At times it was so gross. My throat hurt. I coughed. Nobody appreciates the ability to breathe, and they shouldn't, but I do. I experienced a medical breakthrough. Now I breathe easier. It is amazing not to have to try.

MAGDA Nathaniel experienced his senses differently: he never had the experience of losing functionality. He didn't go from breathing easily to needing a trach; he didn't lose his hearing. Instead, he was always on a path from restriction to freedom. And isn't that what growing up is about for everyone? A baby goes from drinking milk to baby food to solids. Nathaniel went from being fed through a tube to eating real food. Every child has to learn to be careful of his body, to watch out for hot stovetops, to stay out of the street, to hold his breath under water.

Our son had a few additional items on that checklist, but the process, the growing self-awareness and self-care, was a familiar path. That's how I saw it and that's how we talked about it in our house. Nathaniel wasn't a victim. None of us were. That wasn't part of his or our family's identity.

Nathaniel is finally normal, and by normal I don't mean "like everyone else." I mean normal as an absence of need, an absence of special attention, an absence of fragility. He still has differences. I don't care that he looks different. I don't care that he still has a hearing aid. The trach caused the most illnesses and interventions and stress. The trach was what kept him furthest from normal. From day one, when he was born and they talked about the trach, and then he got it, the rest of our family took a giant, thirteen-year-long step away from ease. (Fewer years for Jacob, who was only eleven, but Nathaniel-with-a-trach was all Jacob had ever known.)

As for me, I was done with chemo. My hair was growing back in. I hadn't gotten official word that I was cancer-free, but I knew in my head and my heart that I was fine. If my sicknesses were reactions to Nathaniel's worst moments—getting his brain poked by a doctor; flatlining after the Big Surgery—then my healing would follow his. Now we were both better. A double celebration.

It wasn't just Nathaniel who had stepped into a new realm. It was all of us.

PART VII

A NEW NORMAL

Gift from God

MAGDA   We called Nathaniel's thirteenth birthday party the "Ding-Dong My Trach Is Gone" Party. We hadn't been in Seattle long enough to make a lot of friends, but we invited the two boys who had showed Nathaniel around school. Hunter, a friend of Nathaniel's from Reno, came to stay for the week. The Tremblay family came—Jacob, his sister, Erica, and his parents. Jen, the woman who helped us find a house, brought her two boys. Jacob invited his friend J.P., who was the first friend that he made in Seattle.

At first the kids played with Nerf guns. Then the game truck that Nathaniel had requested arrived and all the kids disappeared into it until it was time for cake. Nathaniel ordinarily didn't like having "Happy Birthday" sung to him, but that year he let it slide. Thirteen is a milestone birthday, and I always loved checking off milestones. Nathaniel had been through more than most, but he was in a game truck with all the other kids, and you can bet he wasn't thinking about one surgery or another. He was probably completely focused on whether he was dominating Super Smash Bros. IV.

NATHANIEL When I was filming the special for National Geographic's show *Taboo*, I was running at the playground and I ran face first into a metal pole. It hurt and I cried. I asked them not to put it in the show. But they put it in anyway, and they edited it to make it seem like I was crying because someone said I looked ugly. They named the episode that I was part of "Ugly."

Filming *20/20* was a very different experience. They were honest and respectful. They looked at our whole experience, instead of squeezing it into an idea they had of what my experiences and feelings should be.

MÁGDA The *20/20* cameras had been with us periodically leading into Nathaniel's Big Surgery, afterward, and throughout my cancer treatment. Nathaniel and I were in the homestretch of our medical issues.

The *Wonder* movie would soon be released, and they were nearly done filming us for *20/20*. The producers wanted Elizabeth Vargas to do one final set of interviews with us, and for some reason they wanted to tape them in Los Angeles. We agreed, and when I texted the *Wonder* movie producer, Todd, to tell him we were coming to town, he said, "If you stay an extra day, I can get you three tickets to the *Beauty and the Beast* premiere!"

The first day we were in Los Angeles, we spent a whole day talking to Elizabeth at a house in the low hills that cradle the city. The crew kept telling us, "We rented this house on Airbnb, but we have a different house where we'll be this afternoon. We want pictures of Nathaniel and Elizabeth walking, with the sunset in the background." Going to a different house just for a sunset sounded a little excessive, but we figured they knew what they were doing.

Later that day, they loaded us into SUVs. A camera crew filmed us on the drive to the second house. This was also odd—why did they want footage of us driving?—but we figured this was their last chance to make sure they had everything they needed. We arrived at a neighborhood with armed guards at the gates. Strange. And we pulled up to a gorgeous house.

The producers said, "Look at this beautiful house. We're going to film you here. But don't get out of the car yet. We want Elizabeth to greet you and walk you to the door."

At this point it seemed clear there was something going on that they weren't telling us. I looked at Russel. He shrugged. "TV," he mouthed to me, and we walked to the front door.

Elizabeth opened the door and welcomed us, which was weird because we'd seen her literally five minutes before. She said, "It's been so wonderful working on your story, that we wanted to give something back to you."

NATHANIEL   It was the nicest house I'd ever seen. A mansion. A glamorous woman came into the room. I could tell she was someone important based on where we were and how everyone was reacting.

Dad leaned down and whispered, "This is Christina Aguilera, the famous star."

I knew the story about how her song "Beautiful" had inspired my parents, and I knew the song.

"You are beautiful, no matter what they say . . ."

MAGDA Christina Aguilera led us to her living room. There was a fireplace, white furs on the sofas, gold decor, a grand piano.

She already knew our whole story. She'd read the letters that Russel wrote to Nathaniel on every birthday, and she knew the story of the night of his birth.

We talked for a bit, then she asked, "Would you mind if I sang 'Beautiful' to Nathaniel?"

Would we mind?!

Five feet away from us, in her own living room, with an accompanist on the piano, she sang to us. She was tiny in person, but her voice was powerful. It gave me goosebumps. I thought, *This is the instrument we all have, but not all of us can use it.* Looking at her black enameled piano with clean, classic lines in that grand room, I thought back to the antique piano I learned on at my great-aunt's humble house. It was ornate, with carved legs and other decorative details. Even the music stand had flowers carved into it. The music I played, on that piano and afterward, was classical, a very different genre of music. I grew up playing according to what the sheet music said. Bach is meant to be played the same way every time. The music that he composed instructs you when to be loud or soft, fast or slow. When I played, I followed the rules. When Christina sang, she had a freedom of performance that I had never experienced. It was as if she and the pianist were having a conversation. They were looking at each other, supporting each other, and while she sang, he was talking with his hands.

Becoming Nathaniel's mother took me off the sheet music. When he was born, I had books telling me the right things to do in the first year of my baby's life. The day I brought Nathaniel home from the hospital, I threw them out. Both Polish and English editions. There was no way to apply the normal baby books to raising Nathaniel. I had to improvise every day. It wasn't comfortable for me, but I had come to embrace the challenge. It was a different kind of music.

As Christina sang, Nathaniel held the Grammy she'd won for that very song, and Russel and I were transported back to the moment we had accepted Nathaniel as a gift from God. And this moment, in the present, was itself another gift from God.

NATHANIEL The meaning that song held for my parents wasn't the same for me. After all, I was just a newborn when they heard it. It didn't change how

I felt about me. But her voice was the most beautiful voice I'd ever heard. This famous adult was standing next to her piano, singing to me, pointing at me when she said "you," looking straight in my eyes. A superstar. It was crazy. It caught me off guard. I was a little overwhelmed.

MAGDA   As we walked out of Christina Aguilera's house, Russel said to Nathaniel, "Dude, what do you think? That was insane!"

Nathaniel asked, "What did I do to deserve this?"

Russel said, "The fact that you asked that question is exactly why you deserve it. You don't even realize."

Nathaniel doesn't see himself as a kid who's been through that much, and he accepts what he's had to endure. This makes us feel like he deserves everything good that comes to him. But he's right in that he isn't the only kid who's been through a lot. There is no way to even out the gifts and struggles we are handed. But we hope his life impacts the world for good.

The next day, we dressed up nicely for the *Beauty and the Beast* premiere, which was a matinee. We took photos with the boys, feeling very Hollywood, then left Russel behind at the hotel since we only had three tickets. We watched the movie with Todd's family, dazzled by the film and how special it was to be among the first to see it. But, for all the glitz and glamour and tears and miracles, the best moment on our trip to Los Angeles was when we took the kids to the Santa Monica Pier. We rented bikes and rode along the beach. The boys were all big smiles. I felt the wind in my hair, the ocean breeze, the warm sun on my head. I had the tiniest pixie cut possible, not even an inch of hair, but I'm gray so it was dyed platinum blond. Nobody passing by would know what a journey we'd had or how special it was for us to be on a trip together for pleasure, not surgeries. We just looked like a family of four, enjoying a relaxing vacation. A normal thing that normal families do. We all had scars, but this was as close to normal as we got, and it was good enough for me.

NATHANIEL Over the months, whenever I was interviewed for *20/20*, I tried to do my best to answer their questions well. They were expecting me to have intense emotions about everything I went through, which made it harder. I don't have deep thoughts about all of my experiences. In reality, I went through it without feeling anything good or bad. I just went through it. I'm always asked about bullying, staring, *Wonder*, Auggie.

How do you feel similar to Auggie?

I know what the right answer to that is. "When I read about Auggie, it's like my own story springing to life on the page." But the real answer is I still don't understand why people associate me with him so much. Yes, we both have Treacher Collins. That means there are basic similarities. But the similarities are all physical. They aren't actually personal. Auggie is a fictional character created by an adult, and I'm me. It makes sense to look for the connections, but it's kind of like trying to dig for diamonds in a sand hill. You're not going to get much more from me than a pile of dirt. But if you're looking for shells, you might unearth all different shapes and sizes.

A New Normal

NATHANIEL   After Mom and I were both better, we decided that our family would stay in Seattle. We had moved around a lot, and we all wanted to stay in one place for a while. I was too fragile for school for a while—and there were lots of complications—so I was homeschooled for several months, but the whole thing took a year, as promised. I went back to school in March of seventh grade. I'd done most of sixth grade in Reno, so in Seattle I was the new kid, showing up post-surgery, finishing out the school year with a bunch of strangers. I wanted to finish the year being homeschooled, but my parents said no.

This time Dad and I didn't write a letter to prepare my classmates. *Wonder* had done that work for us. And, as seventh-graders, we figured they should be able to handle me, and we were right.

Even so, on the first day I felt like I had walked into a movie theater when the movie was nearly over. I was clueless in all my classes. The kids all knew each other. There was no real recess where I could make friends. If they finished lunch early, some kids went to an outside area, but it was just a basketball court, which was not my thing, so I went to the library to read or do homework.

For the first time in my life, I didn't have a nurse shadowing me. It was only when I stopped having one that I realized what it was like to be independent. I was so used to being followed. The nurses were okay, but it was never part of the job description that they had to talk to me or be fun. Mostly they were one more way in which I was a little bit different.

After a few weeks things at school got better. In Language Arts I sat next to some kid I didn't know. I was chilling since I still didn't have friends. Andy was wearing a Pokémon shirt, so we got into a conversation about that. Then I think Andy was trying to get at the fact that I have Treacher Collins but didn't know how, so he said, "I'm Andy. I have Asperger's." I think mentioning his own disorder was Andy's way of saying, "I'm different too." We had that in common.

"Cool," I said. We started talking about random stuff like Minecraft, and, just like that, Andy became my best buddy.

I started knowing my way around the school, I (mostly) caught up on schoolwork, and Andy and I spent hours after school playing video games and inventing superhero fantasies.

Andy has a cat named Bella who isn't very nice— she even gave Andy an exclamation point–shaped scar, but Andy loves this mean cat. Once, his grand-parents came to visit him and brought their blind, deaf dog, who was also losing his sense of smell. If a dog can't smell, hear, or see, it can't do anything. Going around the house was impossible for him. So the dog was stumbling around and Bella kept pouncing on him. He was a tiny dog, smaller than Bella, and was terrified when he lost his balance. I felt so bad for him. It took a minute for me to connect his state to how I was during the Big Surgery. It was a sorry state, but I never thought of myself as pitiful. Maybe that old dog didn't either.

The end of the school year couldn't come quickly enough, and then it was summer. Sum-mers had never been fun for us, but that summer being trach-free opened up the world more than I expected. For instance, being in a windy situation had always been unpleasant for me. One time, at a playground with my cousin Hayden, the wind rushed into the trach, overloading it with air. There was so much air I couldn't breathe. If I closed the trach, I had to breathe harder to get enough air. Before my surgery, I wasn't sitting around moping over the wind and its effects. I never thought, *Hey, I should go through surgery to change the shape of my face so I can hang out on a windy day,* but it was a nice improvement.

The best change came about the day that I beat Jacob in a boxing match for the first time. We like to box on our trampoline, but obviously it would have been bad if he punched me in the trach, so he was never allowed to hit me above my chest, which made it kind of boring. And I still couldn't win because he easily blocked my punches. I'd only ever won once, on a glorious wet, slippery day. But this time, I somehow made him slip and trip. At the time he admitted I won, although later he would claim that he let me win. I just said, "That's right, kid." I'm pretty sure in our next fight I will actually win.

I swam all that summer, sometimes at Beaver Lake, and sometimes at my cousin's pool. At my cousin's I liked to go down in the deep end and push off the bottom. Wearing my goggles, holding my breath, my normal breath, the breath that came in through my nose, and going underwater for as long as I wanted . . . Swimming is the opposite of boring. My life didn't change; I was still me. Maybe you could say it was kind of like having a broken leg your whole life and getting the cast off.

MAGDA   Nathaniel is blasé about the changes in his life, but, as his mother, life changed dramatically the day his trach went away: thirteen years of everything that was required to take care of a foreign part of his body. We had a closet full of medical supplies that I would never need again. I donated some of the sealed boxes to myFace, hoping there was no secret squadron of cockroaches hidden within.

This is strange to admit, but I still keep a good stock of supplies in the laundry room, where nobody goes but me. On the top shelf I have a bag containing everything he needed to have at school: the Ambu bag—a device to help him if he stopped breathing, containers for the suction pump, suction catheters, a hose for the pump, a spare trach, and antibacterial soap. The Ambu bag was so critical, and now it's getting dusty on the shelf. It makes no sense to keep these things. They can't even be attached to Nathaniel anymore, but I can't seem to let them go. They were my safety line, and deep down I guess it's hard to believe I'll never need them again.

Life with a hole in your neck is dangerous. All I ever wanted was for my children to be safe. The effort required to keep Nathaniel safe on a daily basis was constant. Now he is as safe as anyone else.

I tried to make his life complete in spite of the medical interruptions. He started school with everyone else his age. He learned to ride a bike and tie his shoes and make friends and play with dogs and deal with disappointment. He couldn't swim, but I took him to the water anyway. He experienced the pool and the ocean and pushed his own limits.

Dr. McCarthy had given us the piece of advice that proved most important: to give him a real childhood. Russel and I often talked about this when we allowed Nathaniel to do "risky" things like play at the playground, go to the beach, or ride a bike. He had the biggest life he could within his constraints. I was happy that he was alive, and that the trach helped him live. But I was happier without the extra worries and stress.

When Nathaniel had a trach, he couldn't take a shower. Now Nathaniel, at thirteen, had to learn how to wash his hair by himself. It was a moment. I said, "You're all healed up. Tonight, you're going to take a shower, and you're going to do it alone. This is how you do it. Take this much shampoo. Massage your hair and head. Then rinse." At first he wasn't even used to the sensation of giving the top of his skull a good scrub—I always had to keep it careful and gentle, going part by part, very slowly so water didn't drip. It was hard for me to let go of worrying about the shower, even though there was literally nothing that could happen. By habit, I found myself knocking on the door every time he was in the shower to ask if he was okay. You can imagine how he felt about that.

Nathaniel could shower on his own. It was another milestone to check off the list, like riding a bike or tying his shoes—another way in which we were both free.

Nathaniel started eighth grade and Jacob started sixth so they were together in middle school. It was the first time in a while that they had been in the same school. Jacob, now my court reporter, came home and said, "Mom, I've been watching Nathaniel and he's been chewing on his sleeve. Can you tell him not to do it?" Or: "I saw him at lunch. He was eating like a slob." Although he would never judge a kid who was different, Jacob wants Nathaniel to fit in as best he can, to be "cool." Nathaniel does not care. He's a minimalist, which is a nice word for lazy. In eighth grade he still wouldn't tie his shoes because it was too much work. He'd been wearing Crocs and socks exclusively for about six years. Literally. I bought him cool boots, $85 Timberland boots that Jacob was coveting, but he wouldn't wear them because he would have to tie them.

Nathaniel said, "You're trying to make me look cool, Mom. I don't want to look cool. I'm fine with whatever I'm wearing. I don't need clothes to feel better about myself." That was his excuse. Even if the real reason for not wearing those shoes was pure laziness, it was hard to argue with him.

Jacob chimed in to say, "Nobody wears Crocs anymore. You're in eighth grade."

But Nathaniel said, "I don't care, Jacob. Mind your own beeswax."

For Halloween that year, Nathaniel was Vegeta, a character from the *Dragon Ball* manga series. He went to school in costume. Jacob reported that there was a Halloween parade in the gym, during which everyone had a chance to take a solo moment up on the stage. He told us that most of the eighth-graders chose not to join the parade, or they ran on stage, then quickly ran off. But Nathaniel came on stage cheering and dancing and hamming it up. Nobody else had the guts to go all out, but Nathaniel didn't care what anyone thought, and you could tell everyone was happy for him. Jacob told us his brother was smiling ear to ear.

I thought back to all the school plays where Nathaniel was happy to be on stage. He had played the troll in *The Three Billy Goats Gruff* and a bully in another play. In choir concerts he liked to be front and center. I guess he inherited the pleasure I get from being seen and heard.

That October, when my parents came to visit, I took them to see the Grand Canyon. I brought Jacob, but we didn't want Nathaniel to miss any more school. Another stop on the trip was Las Vegas, where I surprised them with tickets to see the magician David Copperfield. We had watched his shows on TV in Poland with great amazement, so my parents were delighted to see him live. We sat right by the stage. The show was about to start when a side door opened. A woman came up to us with a tray of champagne flutes and chocolate-covered strawberries. There was a note on the tray from Russel. It said, "Magda, you are cancer-free. The doctors just called and your scans came back clean!"

The whole theater could see us sitting by the stage receiving this hand-delivered treat. My parents came from such a small town in Poland. It was a spectacular, over-the-top way for them to receive the best news imaginable. They'll never forget it.

The "Real" Wonder Boy

NATHANIEL In November, not long after Hallow-een, our family went to Los Angeles for the *Wonder* movie premiere. We got to ride in a limo to the movie theater, which was cool, and when we got out of the car we were on the red carpet, except it was white, and there were tons of photographers shouting, "Nathaniel! Over here! Over here!" to get me to look at their cameras. I was in shock, and it was a little creepy. How did so many people know my name? Why would people take the time to yell at a kid just to get him or her to look at the camera? There were lots of flashing lights.

MAGDA Just before we went to the premiere, I started feeling guilty. Our family had already gotten to film the *20/20* show. We'd been on the set of the movie. I felt privileged and honored to be included, but before we left Seattle I said to Russel, "There are other kids who would love to have this experience. I want other kids to have a chance." It was the same thing I'd said to Todd when they were looking for an Auggie actor—"Did you interview other children too?" My son isn't more special than any other kid with Treacher Collins, except to me. I wanted it to be fair, and I worried that people would think, "What did this kid do to be treated like royalty? Why can't we go?" Lots of families have their own challenges and their own stories to tell.

Russel said, "There's no way to include everyone. Just be humble. Let Nathaniel have this. It's the only upside to all he's been through. Take the moment. Be grateful." So that's what I did, and later I was happy to see that other kids with craniofacial differences had been invited and were attending the premiere.

We were the first people to arrive at the premiere. Nothing is an accident in Hollywood—the timing had clearly been planned, probably by *20/20*. We were being driven in a big Escalade with tinted windows. The car stopped, and the *20/20* cameraman hopped out and ran ahead to get ready. The car doors opened, and Nathaniel stepped out onto the (white) red carpet. For twenty minutes the media went nuts, yelling Nathaniel's name and snapping pictures of us. For the first three minutes of this Russel was hiding off-camera, sobbing. My heart was beating fast, not with nervousness, but with an excitement that felt oddly familiar. It was another performance. Now I wasn't the center of attention, but my kid—our family—was.

Russel composed himself and we posed, documenting for all time the brief but enormous popularity of dabbing.

When Nathaniel was born, I thought it was the end of the world. On our walks, I threw a blanket over his stroller so as not to draw attention. Now, at a moment when I was standing proud, he was too, saying, *Look at me, people. I made it. I'm not embarrassed by who I am.* A moment in the spotlight meant something different to Nathaniel than it would to an actor or to a kid with no noticeable differences. It was a moment when everyone was looking at him, but they weren't staring at him. They wanted his picture. They appreciated how he looked for all the guts it represented. It was awesome.

During the movie itself, Russel cried again, from the moment the screen went from black to color until the screen went from color to black.

NATHANIEL   The movie was perfect. I wanted it to go on forever. We'd seen them making it and now we saw what we'd watched them make turned into such a cool movie. I especially liked the parts where things were going well, when Auggie is interacting with his friend Jack Will, when they're playing imaginary games and sword fighting. I guess it's the same thing I do in my own life: focus on the good moments.

MAGDA   The hardest part for me was when Via said, "August is the Sun. Me and Mom and Dad are planets orbiting the Sun." I looked over at Jacob and he was crying, just like his dad. Later, he said that the movie reminded him of how badly Nathaniel used to be treated. He said it hadn't been as extreme as it was in the movie, but Jacob had really noticed how much the unpleasant looks and rude comments decreased when *Wonder*, the book, came out. He said, as he had before, "I think *Wonder* helped me more than it helped Nathaniel."

When I walked out of the theater, I felt like there was good in the world. *Good* triumphs. And *Wonder*, the book and the movie, in real life, in our lives, are helping *good* to win. This was Hollywood, but it was real.

When the movie was released, it was a bloc.
This meant that even more people around the w
would have new understanding of kids with facial di
ferences. We knew from experience that encountering
difference was not natural to young children. So if the
Auggie in the movie had less severe facial issues than
some Treacher Collins kids, it didn't bother us. It made
sense to ease kids into understanding.

R.J.'s goal in writing *Wonder* was to help kids
like Nathaniel, and she succeeded. She truly created a
movement, the movement of kindness. Kids who had
been scary to other kids, or teased for their differences,
were being accepted now, more than ever before. And
the empathy she inspired was not just for the craniofacial community. Her message was to accept anyone
different: people who are in wheelchairs, autistic, trans-
gender, short, tall, large, small; people who have Down
syndrome and other genetic disorders. She humanized
infinite faces. She showed that "normal" is everywhere,
in many different forms. The big picture was amazing.

My mother told me that back in my hometown, at
the supermarket where she buys bread, there is always
a copy of *Wonder* available for purchase. It has reached
that far! Poland is not a diverse country, and if Nathaniel had been born in my town . . . I can't even think

about it. I imagine they would have thought that I had a child with differences because God was punishing me for something. But *Wonder* opened up a window, even in Poland. From what I see in my hometown, people now understand that science plays a hand in genetic disorders.

Nathaniel hasn't been to Poland yet, but *Wonder* has paved the way for the trip we will one day take.

The *20/20* producers named the hour-long documentary about our family "The Real *Wonder* Boy," and timed its airing for one day before the movie was released, as they say, in select theaters nationwide.

The ads emphasized the similarities between Auggie and Nathaniel, but *Wonder* is fictional. Our story had started years earlier, and was different. We hoped that seeing images of Nathaniel wearing the draconian cage in the *20/20* show wouldn't scare people away from the movie, but we wanted his story, different and more medically complex, told too.

NATHANIEL Like I said, I'm not the only "*Wonder* kid" out there. I meet and hear about lots of kids who call themselves real-life *Wonder* kids, and I like that.

I'm not Auggie, but "we're all *Wonder* people" sounds good to me and my family.

The night the *20/20* special aired I was nervous. I hoped they didn't have footage of me crashing into anything or crying. I asked them not to film me when I was out of it after the big surgery—it's always weird to see yourself in weaker moments, and it's not who I am.

My mom was crying as we watched. Daddy cries a lot, but Momma doesn't cry often. I patted her on the head and kept watching to see if they'd gotten any good footage of my puppies. There was one scene where you could see Snowball wagging her tail. As you might imagine, that was my favorite part.

MAGDA Jacob and Russel were at a lacrosse tournament, where they watched the *20/20* special with Jacob's entire team in the lobby of the hotel. Nathaniel and I went to a friend's house. I had a knot in my stomach. I had no clue what they would show. Had they edited the big surgery out in order to emphasize the parallels between Auggie and Nathaniel? Was reality too graphic for the general audience?

It turned out that I loved the way they put every-thing together, a story evolving from our initial shock and fear of the unknown, through all the sacrifices, to a final moment at the *Wonder* movie premiere, when Nathaniel turns to the camera and gives a beautiful smile. It gave me chills.

The combination of "The Real *Wonder* Boy" documentary and the *Wonder* movie release did lead to people on the street making the connection between Auggie and Nathaniel more than ever. They would come up to Nathaniel and say, "Oh, you are the *Wonder* boy." He or I would politely correct them: *Wonder* is about every kid who has a craniofacial condition.

But as time passed and Nathaniel healed from the last surgery, his face was less dramatic and people didn't stop in their tracks anymore. Unsurprisingly, this development doesn't make a difference to Nathan-iel. He knows who he is. He still doesn't care what other people think.

NATHANIEL Sometimes people approach me and say they recognize me from TV, and I still get stares from little kids. But now it feels like only 5 percent of people notice me in public places. Which is a good thing.

Gratitude

MAGDA   When Nathaniel was two weeks old, there was a baby who joined him in the hospital. He had many of the same problems as Nathaniel, plus a cleft lip and palate, which means that his lip and the roof of his mouth didn't form properly. The mom didn't speak any English, so there was a translator helping these new parents navigate the complicated medical planet onto which they'd just been teleported. The baby got a trach and a g-tube right away. The mother came to visit him every day.

Over the years, until both of the boys were nine or ten years old, I crossed paths with this family at the hospital. The boy had many of the same surgeries as Nathaniel, but his were covered by Medicaid, health insurance provided by the US government, because the parents had low or no income. Each time the parents returned, they had more children in tow, which to me said that they were in need of even more help from the government. They had the babies, a translator, the surgeries—all the expenses we had and more. Meanwhile, we ended up living in a basement because Russel's income wasn't low enough to qualify for Medicaid, and we still couldn't afford the medical bills.

It didn't seem right to me that Russel would work so hard and this family would get a "free ride." I was so mad that I called President Bush's office! Using a dictionary, I wrote out what I was going to say. To the woman who answered, I recited, "It's unfair that some people with Medicaid get health care for free. My husband was born in this country, and we can't afford a simple apartment. We are living in a basement, because we have huge medical expenses. These people don't even speak English and they get a free ride." That was all I could see.

The woman on the other end of the line listened politely, and said, "I'll get the word to Mr. President."

I'm not proud that I made that call. Over the years, my view changed. When I look back, I see that no matter what bad luck we had, Russel always managed to land a better job. When we couldn't afford an apartment, we had generous relatives who welcomed us to their basement. We had friends and colleagues who gathered together to play golf and raise money for Nathaniel's expenses and myFace. We had the education and resources and connections to stay on our feet, to move forward when we could, and to make our lives better little by little.

This family had all of our troubles but none of that support, none of those opportunities.

Some people are not given a chance to make the most of their lives. Just like my parents. They weren't lazy or stupid. Their options were limited. And I learned so much from my mother, a simple woman who never graduated from college.

Now when I look back, I thank God that this family was able to get the help they desperately needed. I wouldn't change anything. Just because I didn't have what I needed didn't mean they shouldn't have it.

When I see immigrants, I know that they came here for a better life. I respect that. I moved here from another country to marry the American I loved. I was able to move from state to state so Russel could climb the ladder of success and we could have a better life. Why shouldn't someone else move from country to country? Who am I to judge who is worthy to thrive in America? After all these years, thankfully, I want everyone to get help. What would happen to a kid with Treacher Collins without any personal or government resources? What would have happened to that sweet baby? The people who don't have a chance need our help.

My cancer is in remission, which means that it is gone for now, and maybe forever. I say to myself, *This experience did not break me. Because of it, I am thriving as a person, as a mother, as a woman.* I watch what I eat. I watch what I do. I pay attention to how my whole family treats our bodies because I faced the possibility that I might not get the chance to live and care for this body that I have.

After moving around the country chasing jobs and doctors, we have settled in Seattle, where I teach exercise classes and take our four dogs for long outings at the dog park. (We added Coda during my cancer treatment. My excuse was that I wanted to have two male dogs and two females. For balance, of course.) Our backyard has wild rabbits that burrow holes in the lawn and drive the dogs mad. I love to mow the lawn. I know where to be especially careful, where the rabbits might be hiding.

NATHANIEL I am trach-free. I've started taking martial arts with Jacob. The class is awesome, although I never realized how hard it is to do a pushup. I guess I never tried! I've been practicing at home and getting promoted to higher belts because eventually I want to become a black belt and a spy. I'm also studying to become a bar mitzvah. I want to do it, but I have trouble balancing the work with school. I'll be 15 years old this year, and I'm doing it at the same time as Jacob. Instead of a big huge party, we're planning to go to Israel along with our cousin, Hayden.

MAGDA Nathaniel's medical journey isn't over. The bone structure of his face does not grow with the rest of his body. His jaw will just stay where it is. He'll stop growing at around eighteen, when he'll have one more jaw surgery. He'll need a couple of procedures to keep his airway open. We'll try again to give him cheekbone implants to protect his eyes. And he desperately needs some dental work.

The hurdles ahead seem like easy, rolling hills. And if there are surprises, as there are bound to be, none of us are strangers to that possibility.

Just recently, Russel took Nathaniel in for a follow-up appointment with Dr. Hopper. He called afterward to say, "Dr. Hopper said he'd like to see us in a year."

A year. Two summers ago, Nathaniel was going to a doctor's appointment almost every day. A year feels like a lifetime.

A day later I went to see my new oncologist, Dr. Smith. Sadly, my previous doctor had lost his battle with a brain tumor. I grieved him as one can only grieve the person who has saved your life.

At Dr. Smith's office, I spent four hours going from one floor to another, having various tests done. At the end of all of this, Dr. Smith showed me a preliminary report. He said, "This is a miracle. Your blood does not show signs that you had cancer or chemo. You are the healthiest person I've ever seen. Keep doing whatever you're doing."

Then, unbelievably, he said, "I don't want to see you for another year." The exact same words that Nathaniel's doctor had spoken. Two clean bills of health.

The attention I used to give Nathaniel was physical. Now that I'm done cleaning and caring for him, he still gets plenty of attention, especially on the drive to tae kwon do. He talks to me about characters from video games. A lot. It's slightly better than hearing about Thomas & Friends. But he also tells me about his dreams of being a veterinarian. He wants us to have a business together. He'll be the vet and I'll be the groomer. He's convinced it's going to happen. Either that, or he'll be a spy. Two very different jobs, but he's got plenty of time to figure it out.

Jacob has his own transition to make. Looking out for Nathaniel, being responsible for his brother's well-being, has been part of his life, just like being born with Treacher Collins is part of Nathaniel's. Between his brother's surgeries and my cancer, Jacob grew up accustomed to worrying. That habit doesn't disappear overnight. He's still haunted, even by minor things, and when he gets stressed out about a test or some everyday issue, he has flashbacks to the scariest moments with me and Nathaniel. In a way, it's his turn to process everything. As he says, "I'm a bit scarred. But, like Nathaniel's scars, mine give me character." Unlike Nathaniel, Jacob wants to live far away from us when he grows up, in North Carolina or San Diego. He wants to be an oncologist researching a cure for cancer.

Sometimes I ask my kids what heaven would be for them, if heaven is a moment in which you would happily live for the rest of forever. Jacob says that for him heaven is being on the lacrosse field with his team-mates. Nathaniel says, "Being in my room, playing with Legos, with the dogs staring at me." My heaven is taking a nap and being surrounded by the beating hearts of the dogs. Snowball on my head, Brownie and Smokey next to my thighs, and Coda next to my heart.

NATHANIEL Around kindergarten or first grade, I saw the movie *Shrek* for the first time. I was already obsessed with superheroes, and Shrek rose above them all. A major part of the story is that Shrek, who is fat and green and dirty, is portrayed as a hero. He likes the way he looks, and only when the classically beautiful princess is transformed into her true ogre self does he love her. It's been suggested to me that, as a little kid, identifying with Shrek was the easiest way for me to embrace the idea that I didn't have to be perfect on the outside to be a good guy. It's a clever idea. It makes sense. I get it. Shrek equals me. But people around me want everything to be about my differences. Can't I just love a great movie? *Shrek* has an 88 percent approval rating on Rotten Tomatoes. Maybe I'm just part of that 88 percent. People look to Treacher Collins as the characteristic that defines me, but I don't see everything through that lens. I don't even wear glasses (yet).

It's weird for me to write this book, about what I've been through, when I don't want people to think about what I've been through. We like to categorize people. That's how *Wonder* helped people understand me. "Oh, there's a kid like Auggie." But I think all of us have parts of our identity that we'd prefer people to see *through*. You notice how I look? Fine. You have a question or two about it? Sure, okay. But after that, I'd like us to move on, so we can see if we like to play the same games or talk about the same things.

The biggest message of *Wonder* was to appreciate differences, to choose kindness. But there's another message under that one that people may not realize. You didn't want anyone to be mean to Auggie because you liked Auggie. You liked him for who he was, what he and the people around him told you about life in his shoes. Reading about him, it was easier not to be distracted by his appearance. Of course you could see him in the movie, but still, you get my point. That's part of what I hope people take away from my story, the value of separating *who someone is* from *what he looks like*. If this doesn't come to you naturally, if you have to think about it first and remind yourself *looks don't matter, looks don't matter,* I don't see anything wrong with that.

Mostly, I avoid talking about my medical experiences. It's not because remembering brings back any kind of trauma. But my surgeries already took up so much of my time, and they all blend together, so I don't have very many specific stories, or much to say about the unpleasant need to be fixed. I'm definitely an expert on what it's like in a hospital, and how a basic surgery goes, and my recent big surgeries are fresh in my mind, but the ones before that have faded and blurred together. Chances are that by the time I'm thirty or so, when doctors, hospitals, infections, and all that is in the past, the memories will be even smaller and more insignificant.

If your body works, be grateful. You don't have to think about it, spend time on it, work on it. We take it for granted that we're born with everything. I appreciate breathing. I had to have surgeries so that I didn't have to think about it. It's a challenge to appreciate what you already have. You have so much more than you realize.

Our family has gone through more than most people, but we're a "normal" family now. Or maybe we used to be an ordinary family under extraordinary circumstances and now we're an ordinary family under ordinary circumstances. I don't think we ourselves are extraordinary. Except maybe my mom, because she did so much of the worrying, and she had to deal with medical stuff that really grossed her out. That was pretty heroic. Either way, who I am will never change. Treacher Collins doesn't define me. What defines us all is how we face the world we've been given. I'm Nathaniel. I'm not normal, and neither are you.

Acknowledgments

MAGDA   I want to thank Hilary Liftin, our amazing partner in taking our crazy life and transforming it into the pages of this book. You have become a dear friend along the way, and your compassion and caring have afforded me the courage to tell our story. Your brilliance and humor brought life onto these pages that I truly hope will inspire others.

Thank you R.J. Palacio for shining a light on the craniofacial community, creating our amazing champion Auggie Pullman, and for the most amazing little blue book that quite simply made life better for people with differences around the world.

Thank you to my amazing mother and father for believing in me, raising me up in the toughest of times, and imbedding in me the strength I needed to endure the challenges life would throw my way.

Heartfelt thank you and appreciation to Dr. Joseph McCarthy. You not only gave us hope right from the start, but thanks to your pioneering work in the field of pediatric craniofacial plastic surgery you have enabled children like Nathaniel to live long, healthy, and fulfilling lives.

Thanks to nurse practitioner and dear friend Pat Chibbaro for the multitude of ways in which you helped us through the darkest of times. Always with a smile and just the right amount of tough love to make sure we stayed the course!

Thanks to Shelley Cohen for checking the NYU voice mail at just the right time and your simple act of kindness that started us down the path that would run through the rest of Nathaniel's life.

Thanks to Dr. Joseph Bernstein of Mount Sinai Hospital. You define the word "mensch." Your humility as a surgeon, your kind heart, and your caring spirit were instrumental in shaping Nathaniel's life.

Thanks to all the NICU and PICU nurses at NYU, Cincinnati Children's, and Seattle Children's. You are our army of angels.

To Dr. Kaalan Johnson: We met you at Cincinnati Children's and fate would keep us together at Seattle Children's. Your tireless commitment to Nathaniel's care and well-being are a gift we will cherish for a lifetime.

The deepest of thanks to Dr. Richard Hopper and your entire team at Seattle Children's. Your gifts as a surgeon are only outshined by your compassion, patience, and absolute dedication to Nathaniel and children like him. You have redefined the standard of care for kids with Treacher Collins everywhere, and thanks to you, *normal* is now a reality.

Thanks to our family members, friends, teachers, and medical professionals for your ongoing love and support throughout our journey. There are too many of you to thank individually, but you know who you are.

To Nathaniel's teachers, thank you for treating Nathaniel like any other kid and pushing him to learn. Because of all of your efforts, he has acquired a thirst for knowledge and learning. A special thanks to Jodi Schoenbachler. We only had you in Reno for a short while, but you and your fantastic teaching partner, Gail Corthell, have left an incredible mark in Nathaniel's memories from elementary school.

Thank you to Daniel Greenberg, our amazing literary agent and Cat Onder, our editor. Your honest feedback and ongoing support mean the world to us.

Thank you to the children and families everywhere who live a life of differences. It is our combined strength and unbreakable bond that enable us all to face our challenges with open hearts and warm smiles. You are true heroes!

I would like to thank my son Jacob. You, my amazing boy, have spent a lifetime taking a back seat. You have spent a lifetime worrying about me and your brother and never once asked, "When is it my turn?" to be the center of our universe. You stood by my side during chemo and ever-so-bravely helped care for me at an age when you should have been singularly focused on your own happiness. You defended your brother at every turn, and like a brave knight made sure that no one or nothing would ever hurt him. You are kind, empathetic, and so perfectly silly. I love you so much, my little angel.

I also want to thank my husband, Russel. You are stronger and tougher than you think you are. You have been our rock right from the beginning of this journey. Thank you for never giving up and facing the challenges with love, logic, and compassion. I love you.

NATHANIEL I would like to thank my mom and dad for raising me with tons of love and the right amount of discipline and giving me all of the opportunities to have a "normal" childhood despite my differences.

I would like to thank all of my doctors and teachers across the country.

And lastly, but maybe most important of all, I would like to thank my four best friends in the world: our dogs, Smokey, Snowball, Brownie, and Coda. You stood guard as I healed, entertaining me for hours on end, bringing a smile to my face, and loving me unconditionally. Having you in my life has made all the difference in the world!